DICTIONARY
OF
DREAMS

DICTIONARY
OF
DREAMS

Annelie Beaton

CAXTON REFERENCE

© 2000 Caxton Editions

This edition published 2000 by Caxton Editions,
20 Bloomsbury Street, London, WC1B 3QA.

Caxton Editions is an imprint of the Caxton Publishing Group.

Printed and bound in India.

CONTENTS

INTRODUCTION

Why do I dream?

How many times have you returned home from a busy day at work, and felt that your brain was too busy or 'full' to think about what has happened that day, let alone to sort the events out and draw any meaning or logic from them for the future? In today's busy and stressful world, you need all your time and energy to concentrate on what is happening *now*.

This is one of the main reasons why you dream. While you are asleep, your brain is sifting through the events which happened and the people you came into contact with that day, or a week ago, or in your childhood. It will try to make sense of all these facts and emotions so that you may wake up feeling as if your life makes slightly more sense than it did yesterday.

Or, that's the theory. Sometimes you wake up puzzled, wondering why on earth you dreamt of your childhood maths teacher dancing a tango with your mother, and feeling less informed than before. This is called **symbolism**. By analysing the symbols listed in this book, which start on page 37, you can start to discover what the strange images mean. For more on this subject, *see* SYMBOLS AND LANGUAGE, page 12.

The Origins of Symbolism

Dreams have been recorded and interpreted for many thousands of years. To some civilisations dream symbolism was very highly regarded as a way of predicting the future or assessing the past and present.

The Ancient Egyptians, Greeks and Romans placed great faith in dreams as a means to gain answers to questions, solutions to problems and even communication with their gods. Native Americans, Chinese and early Christians also believed we could learn much about our souls and spirituality.

Some dream interpreters (or *oneiromantics*, to use their archaic name) were well-known. Artemidorus Daldianus wrote about mystical interpretations of dreams around the 2nd century. Some of what he wrote is still relevant today, including his distinction between universal and individual symbolism. What this means is that a symbol in a dream can have a general meaning for everyone, and also a particular meaning depending on the dreamer and their circumstances. He went as far as to say that if the dreamer was bad or mean, then the dream was more likely to symbolise bad luck for them. If the dreamer was good-natured, then good things were symbolised. Similarly, if the person dreaming was poor, he claimed that the events in their dream represented less important events in waking life than, say, a wealthier person. Much of his writing, however, concentrated on the fortune-telling potential of dreams. Modern interpreters tend to concentrate on what dreams can tell us about our past or present, but they do believe that an individual's life and personal context must be taken into account for dream analysis.

In the 19th century, the astrologer Raphael published the *Royal Book of Dreams*. He claimed to have found it in the form of an ancient manuscript detailing dream interpretation. He believed in the predictive power of dreams.

Sigmund Freud was a very influential figure in the field of psychotherapy and psychoanalysis, and took a keen interest in dream interpretation. It is said that Freud founded the psychoanalytic movement in the late 19th century and made great advances in this area; he was part-credited with the development of free association between dreams and waking life. In 1900 he published *Die Traumdeutung*, in which he claimed that dream symbols often represented sexual desires.

Gypsy Folklore

Many of the symbols listed in this book (*see* page 37) have more than one meaning. Often one of these meanings stems from the collective wisdom of gypsy folklore. Of all dream interpreters, gypsies are probably the best known group. They seemed to demonstrate a knowledge of the subconscious mind that predated psychoanalysis by hundreds of years.

The roots of their interpretations may go back as far as Ancient Egyptian times, but they have been modified and modernised through re-telling as gypsy culture has changed. For example, the **kettle**, a relatively modern symbol, is a good omen in gypsy folklore as it has played such a large part in their lives over the last few hundred years. Some gypsy symbolism seems strange to the modern dream analyst – a **clock** can predict death, for example. This is because some interpretations are based on superstition surrounding particular objects. If you come across such an interpretation, there may also be a modern interpretation and you should read them both to see which fits your situation best.

Contrary Meaning
Gypsies traditionally believed that some dreams meant exactly the opposite of what they seemed to denote. For example, dreaming of **poverty** was said to mean that you were actually being careful and saving money, so that you would *not* fall into poverty. Similarly, dreaming of acting jealously may mean that you are anxious to avoid displaying this characteristic. Similarly, dreaming of being rich may be a warning not to be too extravagant. There may be some truth in this theory, and it doubtlessly gave hope to those worrying about dreaming of unpleasant symbols, and a warning to those with ideas above their station!

Morality
Gypsies were, and probably still are, very moralistic in their dream interpretation. Dreaming of hard work (even in a **work-house**) is often said to predict good luck and prosperity, or at least an honest life; idleness predicts the reverse. Falseness of any sort, such as **wigs** or flashy **jewellery**, means that you should not trust someone, or

that you are acting falsely.

Overindulgence is also frowned upon, so **gluttony** and similar images symbolise trouble, even illness. Dreaming that you have **servants** may suggest enemies of whom you were unaware.

Nature

It is not surprising that many symbols in gypsy interpretation relate to nature, such as **animals,** agricultural symbols or **birds** (a **goose** is said to represent silliness). Most dreams of plentiful farming, or healthy arable land in general, are good omens, as gypsies had a great respect for, and knowledge of, land. Due to their nomadic existence, they rarely owned land, so tended to romanticise agricultural images, such as **grain** or a **harvest**. However, if you dream that the crop is poor or the land is unhealthy, this means bad luck.

Symbols connected with towns and industry, on the other hand, were generally thought to mean bad luck. In addition, and perhaps unfairly, gypsies tended to attach bad connotations to dreaming of traditional feminine tasks such as **knitting**, as it implied that gossip or malicious talk was never far behind!

Christian Symbolism

Symbolism is very important in Christian life and art (as well as in all other religions). the most important and well-known are described below:

The cross: this is the symbol most frequently associated with Christ and, in particular, Christ's suffering. If you dream of a cross it could mean a desire to be more in touch with your spiritual side, or a sign of guilty feelings or sacrifice.

The dove: this is said to be a symbol of the Holy Spirit and also of Jesus Christ. Worldwide it has been adopted as a symbol of peace. Gypsy folklore states that it is a good omen in a dream.

The fish: in primitive pre-Christian times the fish was a symbol of fertility. Christians use it to symbolise Christ as, in ancient Greek, the letters of the word 'fish' spell out the initials of the words *Jesus Christ, the Son of God*. In earlier Christian times dreaming of a fish may have meant that you were conscious of your religion, but it is unlikely nowadays as people do not usually make the connection between the two images.

Symbols and Language

Symbolism is important in language as well as in dreams, and the two can be compared. We use metaphor, a type of symbolism, when writing or speaking, to express ourselves more creatively or interestingly. We might say, for example, 'that man is a cold fish' or 'my car eats money'. Similarly, our dreams can present fantastical images which actually stand for something quite mundane. You may dream that you are being taught the Flamenco by a devastatingly handsome lover, and wake up only to realise that your brain is helping you to remember your Spanish class that day.

We also use certain phrases to avoid hurting someone's feelings or causing offence, e.g. 'He passed away' (he died) or 'I think we should go our separate ways' (I want a divorce). Dreams can also happen this way, showing images which are more pleasant than the situation they represent, such as a bereaved relative appearing then waving goodbye, to reassure you that they are happy. In this way your brain can accept the facts more easily.

SLEEP

What happens when I sleep?

Scientists who have studied people sleeping for many years have identified four main stages that you go through during the sleep process:

1 – In stage one, you grow more relaxed, passing from **conscious** to **unconscious**. Your breathing and heart rates slow down; your eyes start to roll. You start to drift in and out of a light sleep, and can be wakened easily. If wakened, you may believe that you have not yet fallen asleep and were awake all the time. After an undisturbed period in this stage (about 10–20 minutes), you move into stage two.

2 – In this stage you are now asleep, although you can still be woken easily. Your eyes are still rolling, and your breathing gets deeper and slower. This stage lasts about 10–20 minutes.

3 – You are now in a deep sleep. Your **brain waves** slow down and your muscles relax more. Also, your heart rate and breathing slow down further and your body temperature drops. Your eyes may roll from side to side. At this point it is difficult to wake you.

4 – In stage four, you are in the deepest level of sleep.

Brain waves are slow and large, and you growth hormones work to repair tissue in the body. This stage usually lasts for about 20 minutes. The whole cycle from stages 1–4 can take 90–100 minutes and will be repeated several times throughout sleep.

After completing this stage, the sleep cycle goes into reverse, working through stages three and two again. However, when you reach stage one again, things are different. The brain waves and breathing are similar, but now you are in **REM** (rapid eye movement) **sleep**. The majority of dreaming takes place here. If you do dream outwith REM sleep the dream will be more mundane, and will seem more like ordinary thoughts rather than dream images.

REM Sleep

If you are woken during REM sleep it is likely that you will be in the middle of a dream. After about 10 or 20 minutes in this stage you will move back to stage two, three and four, and so on.

Each time you enter the REM stage, it lasts longer. Therefore the last part of the night's sleep is when you will experience your longest and most vivid dreams.

If you are disturbed or woken during REM sleep, you will feel more tired than if you were woken at any other stage. Your body will then try to compensate the following night and try to spend more time in this stage. Scientists have proved that this stage is essential for your well-being, and people who are deprived of it will eventually suffer mental health problems.

Physical Effects

Your muscles are in a sort of paralysis. This is said to happen so that you cannot hurt yourself or move too freely during your dreams, especially if those dreams are frightening or violent. Your eyeballs move rapidly and your hands and/or feet may twitch. You may also talk, shout or laugh. (This accounts for the fact that many people believe that their pets are dreaming when they twitch and whimper during sleep.)

How to get a good night's sleep

In order to remain healthy and alert, and to dream well of course, there are several points worth noting:

1 – How much sleep do I need?

The amount of sleep each individual requires to stay healthy varies. Some need only 3–5 hours, but they are in the minority. The average adult needs between 6 and 8 hours.

When babies are born they can sleep for up to twenty hours; some need a lot less, most sleep for about twelve hours. As you get older this decreases and by old age you need much less sleep than you did as a young adult.

It is up to you to decide how much sleep is best. You can judge by your performance at work, your irritability, your level of conversation, etc. whether you are sleeping enough.

2 – Does eating affect sleep and dreaming?

It is not advisable to eat immediately before going to bed. If your digestion is still working hard while you are trying to sleep, it can disturb your dreams, possibly making them more exaggerated and difficult to interpret.

Certain foods such as cheese and butter are very fatty, and you should avoid them before bed. Also, foods which induce wind (baked beans, raw vegetables, etc.) should only be eaten a long period of time before sleeping, to allow for maximum comfort while dreaming.

Alcohol, drugs and caffeine should also be avoided before sleeping, they alter the natural length of time you normally take to fall asleep, and diminish the quality of sleep. You will usually wake up feeling less refreshed. Sleeping tablets in particular seem to limit REM sleep and thus, although you may sleep more, you will not get the right kind of sleep.

What is advisable is a small glass of water, a herbal tea (such as camomile), or a milky drink.

3 – How does the right environment help?

You should aim to be in bed about half an hour before you want to fall asleep. Try to make your bed as comfortable as possible. One pillow is best (unless a physical ailment demands that you use two) and your duvet or blankets should be neither too heavy or too light. Your bed should be firm but not too hard.

Noise should be kept to a minimum – try earplugs or a relaxation tape to block noise out if necessary. It is beneficial to open a window (just a couple of inches will do) to receive fresh air. A warm bath with a soothing aromatherapy bubble bath (such as lavender) will wind down your muscles and your mind.

Reading is the best way to relax, and you should try to

switch off from stress and calm your thoughts before closing your eyes. Avoid exciting television programmes or films that you won't want to switch off.

4 – What if I can't sleep?

Insomnia happens to around a third of the population at one time or another, and means that you find it very hard to relax and sleep, even if you are very tired.

Exercise, at least two hours before bedtime, does help, as your body will feel more tired, but also more relaxed. Avoid sleeping during the day, even napping, as this can keep you awake for hours past your normal sleeping time. Consciously relax all your muscles from head to foot (you will be surprised at how tense they are), and try to think of something relaxing, such as pleasant childhood memories. A relaxation tape may also help, as it helps you to switch off, and blocks out any noise which may keep you awake. Finally, an eye mask (such as those used for travelling) and ear plugs may feel strange, but they will block out a lot of light and sound.

DREAMS

Recording Your Dreams

Recording your dreams as soon as you wake up helps in two ways. Firstly, it is much easier to remember the whole dream and all the details if you write it down upon waking. Secondly, a series of these dream records can allow you to analyse patterns in your life and thus examine what is really going on and how you feel about events and people.

How to keep your Dream Record

1 – Have a notepad and pen by your bedside at all times. Try to remember everything that happened in your dream as soon as you wake up – the longer you leave it, the less you are likely to remember. Little details are important, as well as the main events.

2 – Note the day, date and time of writing, to enable you to look for patterns (e.g. a dream involving fear every Sunday night may reveal a hidden fear regarding someone at work, for example).

3 – Write down what else is happening in your life, e.g. 'I feel nervous about my interview next week'; 'My brother is intruding in my life again. I feel resentful towards him',

and so on.

4 – If at all possible, try to train your mind to wake before your alarm clock rings. This is difficult to do but can be very beneficial as loud noises may disperse the images in your mind and make it harder to recall your dreams.

Types of Dreams
Through many years of analysis, scientists recognise that there are distinct categories of dreams, apart from just 'normal', factual ones. Some, like **nightmares**, are more likely to happen to children, and **clairvoyant** dreams are more likely to occur in people who are more psychically 'open'. The list of **typical** dreams shows that many symbols and images are common to us all.

Clairvoyant Dreams
This is a rare but extremely powerful and sometimes disturbing type of dream. You dream of something happening and the next day, week or whatever, it happens. Some people have been known to predict accidents, meetings, births, even death. It is possible that these people have either shown some sort of psychic powers in waking life, or will become aware of such a power and find that it visits them regularly after the first time. If this happens to you it may be shocking and scary, but people have been predicting in dreams for centuries. Also, many dream symbols are said to have future-telling properties, such as a **sheep** being a prediction of prosperity.

Another way that clairvoyance *seems* to manifest itself

is that you dream of something which you could not possibly have known. For example, you may dream that there has been a fire in your neighbourhood. Upon waking, you hear on the news that there has indeed been a fire, only a few streets away. You are amazed that you dreamt this. In actual fact, you may have seen smoke rising from the rooftops before going to bed, or smelt smoke in your dream, and only your subconscious has taken in this fact. This, then, is not actually clairvoyance but actual information which your conscious mind has not yet acknowledged.

Nightmares

Nightmares happen to us all, and can make you scared to even try to sleep, resulting in insomnia. They are most likely to occur if you are a child or an adult female. Children often dream that they are being pursued by things or creatures which they fear the most, such as giants, monsters or spiders. Often this can be triggered by a story they read or listen to before sleeping, so parents should be careful if they recognise a dream image in their child's dream to be a character from a book.

As an adult you can also have nightmares which relate to your deepest fears, such as being attacked at night, or those you love dying or leaving you, being hated by others or perishing in a fire. These fears can be buried from as early as childhood, in which case they will probably be **recurring**, or they may be new fears, prompted by buying a house or starting a new job.

As with recurring dreams, when you confront the

problem, your nightmare should disappear.

Physical Dreams & Stimuli

This is a subject which fascinates dream researchers. Actual physical stimuli can enter your dreams as images and actions.

For example, when you dream of **climbing**, the physical tiredness and lack of breath can actually be due to heart problems or a lack of breath while sleeping.

Dreaming of **falling** may be due to your not being supported on your bed, falling out of bed during sleep, or circulation problems meaning that you cannot feel your limbs.

If you dream that you are **flying**, this can occur as a result of the falling and rising of the chest as your breathe. Also, some people who have been near death but recovered to wake up have reported flying in their dreams, as of they were rising to heaven.

Heights can appear in your dream if you are lying diagonally across your bed with your feet dangling, and this enters your dream as a fear that you will fall off.

Dreaming of being back at **school** is sometimes attributed to your limbs seizing up in cramp while sleeping, and in your dream this appears as the constraint of sitting at a small desk!

Losing teeth can appear as a dream image due to grinding your teeth, hearing someone else doing so, or having dental problems such as toothache.

If you dream that you are **naked**, this can be due to your throwing off a duvet or covers.

Feeling **hot or cold** in your dream is often a result of the temperature in your room.

You may sense that you are **ill** or even **pregnant** and this manifests itself in your dream, either with you seeing yourself ill or pregnant, or seeing one of the many symbols which denote this (*see* the section on DREAM SYMBOLS, page 37).

Recurring Dreams

All dreams contain messages, but recurring dreams are probably the most urgent. The same events keep being replayed again and again, over a period of days, weeks or even years. Two thirds of adults are said to experience recurring dreams at some point. Your subconscious is trying to tell you to deal with a situation that you are ignoring. There can be several reasons for this.

You may have had a traumatic experience in childhood, and rather than dealing with it, have tried to suppress it deep within your mind. You may have had a bullying parent or relative, or a strict upbringing, or perhaps a bad accident. Whatever it is may be replayed in your dreams until you finally confront it.

You may also have a worry which is particularly prevalent at present and will go on for some time. Perhaps you have a teenage daughter or son whom you worry about when they go out at night. Or it could be that you seem to have permanent money troubles. When these troubles go away, the dream should stop.

Recurring dreams can also represent your phobias, such as heights, snakes, etc.

Finally, it could be that you feel that you have not 'finished' a particular situation. Perhaps you rowed with someone close to you and they died or went away before you had a chance to make up. Maybe you still feel hurt after a relationship has finished, and you wish that you could tell the person how they made you feel.

Sexual Dreams

Dreaming of sex is common (*see* TYPICAL DREAMS, page 27) and can be disturbing, as the images are likely to be much more explicit than your waking thoughts about sex. This may mean that you wish to explore your sexuality or fantasies more than you have done so far in your life. It could also mean that there is another aspect of your personality you wish to develop that is nothing to do with sex, such as your creative side.

You may also be worried if you dream of sex with someone other than your current partner, or someone whom you normally find unattractive. It could mean that you do wish to have an affair, or are having one at present. On the other hand, adultery can simply represent guilt of any sort over something you know you shouldn't have said or done.

Teenage males in particular often experience what are known as 'wet dreams', where they dream of sex or associated subjects, and wake up to find that they have ejaculated. This is very common and is the body's way of dealing with new, exciting, but often terrifying, subjects. More than a tenth of adult males' dreams have a sexual image in them, and females about half this amount.

Many images can symbolise sex during a dream, such as **rockets, poles, ladders** (the phallus), or **tunnels** and **bowls** (the female genitals), or **insects** (sexual disgust or confusion). A very common image used in films to represent sex was a train entering a tunnel, so dreaming of this can mean that sex is on your mind.

Typical Dreams

The number of different dreams possible is infinite, as every person has a different life, and different people, things and occurrences in it. However, there are patterns. Scientists and dream analysts now recognise that some symbols and images are universal.

At first glance, the subjects on the list following seem to have nothing in common. But in actual fact there are distinct similarities between many of them. Some, such as **losing teeth, exams/school** and **missing a bus/train** relate to worries we all experience at one time or another. We feel as though we are not knowledgeable enough, or good-looking, or confident. Dream symbols such as **flying** and **climbing** can represent desires: the desire to escape, to do well at work, to be more extrovert.

In other words, typical dreams occur because we all experience the same feelings and worries, and need to process them using one of the simplest and best devices there is: our dreams. Following is a list of the most common images:

abandonment: the dream image of being abandoned is often a very upsetting one. Children frequently have this dream, as they worry that parents or friends will leave them or stop loving them. As an adult you probably still feel this fear too, different ways. Fear of rejection by a peer group, your partner, work colleagues, etc. is very common and so not surprisingly the mind conjures this up in dreams regularly.

aggression: this is a surprisingly common feature in dreams (up to half contain at least one aggressive image). It is unfortunately a common part of life too – if you stopped to think how many angry or rude people you come into contact with on a daily basis, you would not be surprised that aggression played a part in your dreams. Also, there will be many times when you feel angry and aggressive with others, and this will be played out in some way in your dream. You may dream of yourself being aggressive towards others, or they may be involved in some sort of fight which you merely observe.

Aggression can also represent people of whom you are, or have been, afraid, such as a dominant parent or partner, a teacher, or your boss.

burglary: This dream *can* be sparked off by your hearing sounds in your environment while you sleep, but there can also be real fears behind it. Many people have been burgled in real life; it is probably the event that homeowners fear most. No-one likes to have their privacy invaded or lose their possessions.

Burglary can also stand for any other situation where your privacy has been invaded, or any other deeply-felt loss, so a wide range of possibilities can be symbolised by this. In addition, burglars can represent feared or hated people.

captivity: feelings symbolised by captivity can range from problems in a relationship, to feeling as if you are not in control of your life. This dream is particularly common at times of intense frustration, when you feel powerless to do anything to change your situation.

climbing/carrying: we all strive for better things in life, whether material, emotional or spiritual. Climbing indicates a need or desire to get to a 'higher' place than your present one (although this does not necessarily mean status). It most commonly means ambition.

Carrying suggests that you have a burden on your shoulders, and it is common to feel like this concerning a job, or financial problem.

If you dream of puffing and panting, out of breath, there may also be a physical cause such as heart or breathing problems. *See* PHYSICAL DREAMS.

death/dead people: one reason we dream about death so frequently is that we know it will come to all of us but nobody knows what happens when we do die. Also, death is all around us: those we love die, we hear about death on the news and watch it in films.

Missing loved ones who have died is probably the most common cause of dreaming about death and dead people, followed by fear of your own mortality and worry for those who will be left behind. Freud believed that if you dream of loved ones dying and feel no grief, you may actually be wishing for something else in your life to end, such as a relationship or job. Death in a dream may also represent general sadness and problems.

exams/school: the symbolism here is obvious: you feel as though you are being tested and worry that you do not know enough about something. It stems from a basic insecurity that most people have – simply not being good enough. Dreaming about exams and school is most common when you lack confidence or are under extreme pressure – and not just in an educational environment; it is also common among those who work.

Some analysts believe that only people who have failed an examination before will dream of exams, but this is not the case. Anyone who has to prove themselves can have this dream.

See also PHYSICAL DREAMS.

falling: dreaming that you are falling, slipping or sliding often comes at the end of a **flying** dream (see below), and can mean that a feeling of freedom and independence has turned to disaster. This is one of the most common dream images and can be frightening. You will often wake in a panic before you hit the ground, then the next night, start all over again. It can mean that you feel you have let yourself or others down and ruined a potentially good thing. Real disasters or problems can also be predicted.

Freud claimed falling had erotic symbolism, meaning that the dreamer was afraid of sex and possibly too moral to enjoy it. If there is a landing at the end of the fall, this is said to represent climax.

See also PHYSICAL DREAMS.

family: there can be many reasons why you may dream of your family members. There is usually a particular reason why they are on your mind: you have quarrelled with someone; maybe they are having problems that you wish you could solve. Another reason could be that they represent a characteristic that you possess, e.g. possessiveness or generosity. Perhaps you feel that this characteristic is not a good one to possess and your family member appears to 'tell' you this.

Your family can also represent other groups of people. If you dream of a happy family occasion, this generally represents any happy occasion in the future. If your family argue in your dream, this can symbolise an inner conflict with which you have been struggling, or an argument you have had with friends, work colleagues, etc.

flying (without a plane)or floating: this is also a very common dream image. You dream that you are soaring above a city, the countryside, or a group of people, looking down. The main reason that so many people have this dream is that they need to escape restrictions, experience more freedom, and generally live life to the full. in today's stressful world that is rarely possible.

Flying could also represent your sense of spirituality and religion, i.e. the soul rising heavenwards.

It is usually a positive, optimistic dream, meaning that you should feel more free and happy soon, and any money troubles should cease. There is often a sense of extreme happiness and freedom.

See also PHYSICAL DREAMS.

heights: dreams of standing at the top of a cliff, mountain or precipice are invariably accompanied by fear or anxiety. Therefore what this represents is anything that is making you similarly anxious in waking life. It could be fear of failure in your job or exams, a reluctance to commit in a relationship, or a general worry about a change you must make in your life.

If in your dream you fall down from where you are standing, you are probably very worried about losing control, or you feel that you are failing already.

Being stuck at the bottom, looking up at a cliff, precipice or building of a great height means that you feel stuck, and as if you will never scale the heights necessary to reach your goals.

See also PHYSICAL DREAMS.

killing/murder: this is a typical dream image in that most people dream of it at one time or another, but the reasons for it can be vastly different from one person to another. However, the reason is always connected with getting rid of something, or improving a situation dramatically.

You may be angry with the person you dream of killing (although it is unlikely you wish to harm them), or perhaps you are jealous of something they have and wish to take it away.

The person who is killed may also represent a negative aspect of your own character which you wish to lose or suppress. You should ask yourself if you and this person share any traits.

There may also be hidden feelings that you wish to bring to the surface and, in doing so, 'kill' them.

If you are the one who is being killed or murdered, you probably feel that others are holding you back or victimising and oppressing you. The desire to escape can be dramatically replayed in a dream as your death, and therefore your escape from the situation. it is really your subconscious trying to shock you into fixing your problems.

losing teeth: this strange dream image is more common than you may think. Because teeth are so important, losing them in a dream can mean the loss of something important in waking life, such as your youth or looks, or a relationship. If you recall feeling embarrassed in your dream, then this can relate to an embarrassing situation in waking life, or one where you felt you had 'lost face'.

If teeth are bared, this can mean that you or someone you know has been hostile or aggressive.

Gypsies and other traditional dream interpreters believed that losing teeth meant future sadness, even illness.

See also PHYSICAL DREAMS.

missing a bus/train: this is a frustrating event in waking life, so in a dream it represents anything which you have found frustrating, or which you have missed out on. This may be anything from not receiving a promotion you feel was due to you, or letting a relationship go and regretting it.

You may also be feeling very stressed, and believe that you are not performing properly at work. If in your dream you cannot run fast enough to catch your connection, you could be suffering from exhaustion in waking life.

A train is also said to represent sex or sexual desire, so perhaps you feel inadequate in that area.

Seeing yourself on a train can mean that you are

moving house soon, or changing your life in some way. Perhaps you are also missing someone who lives far away.

nakedness: dreams that you are naked generally fall into two types: the dream where you throw off your clothes deliberately, and the dream where you find yourself naked, to your shock or horror.

The first dream usually means that you wish to be less inhibited in waking life, to reveal previously hidden emotions, or to confront and challenge others' perceptions of you.

The second type means that you are worried about other's opinions of you, fearing that they may find out all your faults, and then reject you.

Both dreams may have sexual symbolism: the deliberate undress may reveal a more adventurous streak which you wish to unleash; the accidental undress may mean that you are nervous about sex or unwilling to explore your sexuality further.

See also PHYSICAL DREAMS.

sex: dreaming about sex (often a difficult subject to talk about) is a way to live out fantasies, explore feelings and emotions, and generally do what you want without feeling embarrassed. Also, sexual desire is a basic, common urge which most people feel regularly, so it is not surprising that it features so often in dreams. For more detail, *see* SEXUAL DREAMS, page 26.

water: as so much of the planet you live on is made up of water, you are likely to dream about water in some form in around a quarter of your dreams.

If you dream of the sea, an ocean, or a river, then calm

water generally means happiness in your life, and few problems. Choppy or stormy water means the reverse.

Sometimes the events in your dream actually take place underwater, with everyone in it able to breathe properly as if this were normal, and movements being slow and exaggerated. This usually means that you wish that things in your life would slow down and that you had more time to appreciate the people and things in your life.

If you dream of swimming on your own, especially in deep water, this often means a desire to regress to the womb. You are probably feeling vulnerable and wish to be more protected.

If you dream of being in trouble in the water, this could simply stem from a deep-seated fear of water, or it could also mean that you are having problems which are threatening to overwhelm you. Dirty muddy water means trouble or loss.

DREAMING – THE SYMBOLS A–Z

A

abandonment this is one of our most primitive fears as humans, and to dream of being abandoned by close family or friends may reflect concern as to how others feel about you; you may in life feel unwanted or unloved, even isolated. Dreams of abandonment may also signify a greater freedom in your personal or sexual life. *See also* ALONENESS.

abbey to dream of an abbey, or similar place of comfort, symbolises sanctuary, either finding it or seeking it. *See also* PRIEST.

abduction *see* KIDNAPPING.

abortion if you are a woman dreaming of abortion, this can mean apprehension about a new project.

A man dreaming of abortion usually signifies guilt (although not necessarily of a parental nature).

abroad *see* TRAVEL.

abscess according to tradition, this symbol in a dream is a lucky one, denoting good fortune and/or good health, as generally are boils, or **ulcers.** The reason is that these afflictions result in the body being cleared of impurities and restored to health.

abyss dreaming of an abyss can mean impending danger or a warning to the dreamer. If there is fear involved, you may be failing to face certain situations, or losing control. If there is no fear it may symbolise going further in a certain direction than was previously imagined possible. Often vertigo sufferers may dream of an abyss, for obvious reasons. *See also* CLIFF, FALLING, PRECIPICE.

acacia flower *see* FLOWERS.

accident dreaming of an accident usually indicates anxiety. If you are injured, then it can mean you are punishing yourself for something.

If the accident happens to a person you know, it can symbolise bad feeling towards that person.

If the accident happens while travelling, this may symbolise the end of a long-term relationship.

The dream accident may also simply be due to the trauma of a real accident which has already occurred.

If a specific part of the body is injured in the dream, this may be due to a real injury stimulating the mind.

acorn the acorn is a symbol of growth, and represents the mental or physical growth of the dreamer. The person who dreams of acorns is lucky, as they are also said to symbolise good health and happiness.

adoption if you dream that you are being adopted as a child, this probably means that you are in need of more human contact. *See also* FAMILY.

adultery if you dream of having an adulterous affair, this may spring from guilt about an actual affair, or the desire to have an affair.

On the other hand, it could be that you know someone who has embarked upon an affair, and are mentally sifting through your knowledge of that fact.

A dream of this sort may also have nothing to do with

adultery, but simply with guilt associated with something else.

adventure a wild, adventurous dream usually signifies a desire to escape the mundane parts of life. If the adventure is frightening, you may need to analyse the particular events or symbols separately in order to find out what you need to escape from. Are you falling or running? Is anyone else in your dream? and so on.

aeroplane *see* TRAVEL.

aggression if you are being aggressive, this may denote real-life pent-up anger and you should take note of the person or thing on the receiving end of your anger, as it may reflect real frustrations you need to resolve.

If the dream is of an aggressive woman, this is said to represent a mother, or mother figure, especially if you have a difficult relationship with this person in real life.

If you dream of an aggressive man, then this symbolises fear of another's power. If you are male, then it could more specifically relate to a power struggle with work or money.

alcohol if you dream of drinking alcohol to excess you are probably scared that you will lose control over some area of your life.

If the alcohol is being enjoyed in moderate proportions, it may simply mean that a **celebration** is on the cards.

alien(s) this dream represents fears about your own safety, especially from strangers.

alley the narrow walls symbolise a problem from which you wish to escape. What is at the end of the alley is significant. If you can see no way out you may be feeling trapped by your problem and see no escape. If you walk out at the other end, this signifies a more positive outlook.

alligator *see* **animals.**

almond this is a sacred symbol in the Far East which means that you will travel abroad soon and enjoy life. *See also* FOOD.

aloneness if you have chosen to be alone this signifies a need to think things through, to regain strength, or to gain peace. You may also be breaking away from a group you once belonged to, e.g. growing up, becoming an adult and leaving childhood behind. This is especially true if you are going somewhere alone. *See also* ABANDONMENT.

anchor this is a sign that you may be seeking solidity and strength where it is presently lacking, e.g. in a close relationship. The anchor is also a symbol of hope in Christianity.

angel to dream of an angel is said to be a prediction of help from another source, and inner peace. More than ever, people now report seeing angels while awake; they are a religious symbol of all that is good in an increasingly uncertain world. Not surprisingly, then, the number of people who dream of angels has also increased dramatically. Dreaming of *seraphim*, the highest order of angels, means that you will get in touch with your spiritual side and this will be a very fulfilling experience, according to gypsy folklore.

animals if the animal is domestic, this represents a more homely situation and general happiness.

If wild or untamed the animal may represent your own 'wild side' and your desire to escape restrictions; alternatively it could represent your enemies.

The way the animal behaves is relevant, in the same way as humans' behaviour. Also, all animals have distinct characteristics, so the particular animal you dream of is important too:

alligator or crocodile: you are afraid of an enemy who could be dangerous and cunning.

bear: in your dream a bear might be a big and cuddly protector, in which case it is said to represent a parental figure looking after you, or someone trying to 'possess' you; it might, however, be a ferocious killer which symbolises an enemy.

camel: this is a patient and hardworking animal, used for carrying people and things. Maybe you are carrying a burden in life – for someone else?

cat: seen as mysterious, aloof creatures, cats in dreams may symbolise deceit and underhandedness from one close to you; alternatively, a cat may represent an elegant and independent person. All depends on your perception of cats. A *black cat* is said to be a bad omen, traditionally due to its association with witches. A *kitten* symbolises innocence, joy and happiness. Dreaming of a *wildcat* means that someone in your confidence cannot be trusted, according to gypsy folklore.

chameleon: according to gypsy folklore, this animal symbolises someone who is deceiving you. *See also lizard*, below.

cow: these are placid creatures who give much to mankind; is this how you view yourself/are viewed by others? The *bull* is a more aggressive and/or erotic symbol and may represent lust, a violent enemy or slander. A herd of *cattle* is said to be a sign of good fortune. An *ox*'s nature is more extreme than that of the cow: it is normally yoked and works even harder. Maybe you are making too many sacrifices.

deer: this signifies possible quarrels with your loved one, according to gypsy folklore. If you kill a deer in your dream it is said to foretell of wealth. The *fawn* is a timid, flighty animal and may represent yourself or someone close to you. It also suggests fickleness. A *reindeer* is a good omen, due to its associations with Christmas. The *stag* can be a good omen, signifying success in money matters; it can also symbolise aggression and loneliness.

dog: as with cats, how you feel about dogs is usually revealed in your dream. You may see a loyal, loving creature which probably represents a good friendship or a relation. If your dream dog is fierce, you may in real life be afraid of dogs and so the connection is simple; you may on the other hand be worrying about betrayal by another. To be bitten by one is said by gypsies to mean injury by a friend, although psychoanalysts Jung and Freud said it had erotic symbolism. A *bulldog* is a particular symbol of loyalty and protection. A *mastiff* or other similarly powerful dog symbolises a strong, powerful stranger who will become your friend. If you are bitten by one, however, this means a strong friend will hurt you. If you dream that you are hunting with *hounds* this means a business or other project will not pay off.

donkey/ass/mule: to dream of any of these animals means patience is necessary to overcome hurdles. They are also Christian symbols of humility.

elephant: this symbolises wisdom, especially in India, and great power; maybe you seek these qualities for yourself.

elk: this is said to symbolise good fortune, according to gypsy folklore.

ferret: this animal represents a sly and conniving person, purely based on its reputation (perhaps unfairly!).

fox: this is a cunning and wily animal, so you may see yourself as being cunning and outwitting others, or maybe you have been fooled by another person with these attributes.

frog: the frog is a symbol of new life and rebirth, of making a change in your life. This is generally a lucky dream symbol. if you feel repulsed by or scared of a frog, then perhaps change in making you uneasy but will be for the best. See also *toad*, below.

goat: the goat can be a playful and mischievous creature, maybe representing someone you know! According to the symbolism of Christianity goats are slovenly and wicked creatures, said to represent deceit.

hare: in gypsy folklore, the hare is a clever and resourceful animal and so represents someone who displays these characteristics, perhaps yourself. It also predicts money that money will come your way through your intelligence and resourcefulness.

hedgehog: this is the symbol of an old friend who is honest and kind; perhaps you will meet up with one whom you have not seen for a while.

hog: this represents both sensuality and greed.

horse: a fast and powerful creature, the horse represents energy, whether physical, emotional or sexual. Riding a horse can represent the sexual act, or it can mean you are being carried away by something you can't control. If you are being pursued by a horse, you may be scared to develop your own potential. If a man dreams of a healthy young *mare* this is said to foretell of a happy marriage to a beautiful young woman, according to ancient dream interpretation. If the mare is unhealthy then the marriage will not be a happy one.

hyena: this is a symbol of aggression, and dreaming of one predicts sadness and cruelty.

kangaroo: as with other wild animals, such as the *leopard*, a kangaroo can symbolise worries or problems.

leopard: *see* above.

lion: the king of the beasts is the symbol of power and strength; dreaming of one may mean contact with a great or powerful person. Fighting a lion may mean arguing with an enemy.

lizard: in mediaeval times, the lizard was a sign of bad luck. In a dream it means bad luck too, perhaps due to enemies making things difficult for you. See also *chameleon*, above and *salamander*, below.

lynx: this symbolises an enemy who is watching you.

monkey/ape: dreaming of either of these may signify deceit or bad intentions.

mouse: this means that you or someone close to you may not be asserting themselves as they should.

otter: this represents people you know who may be dangerous or hurtful towards you, according to gypsy folklore.

pig: the pig is seen by some as greedy and dirty, others as clean and loveable. Your perception of them in waking life should tell you what your dream symbolises — a situation or person which is either dirty and unpleasant, or desirable.

porcupine: this prickly creature symbolises a need to tread carefully in business or relationships in the near future.

racoon: according to gypsy folklore, the racoon is a symbol of rain. Some ancient cultures used racoon skins to bring on rain, which is how the symbolism came about.

rat: rats are, perhaps unfairly, hated and feared by many; to dream of rats may reflect your own concerns about being perceived the same way — as a social outcast. You may also fear your home or relationships being destroyed if you dream of a pack of rats.

salamander: in ancient times, these animals were believed to live in fire. dreaming of one means that you will be safe from harm either by enemies or nature.

sheep: these are said to signify prosperity, and to dream of a *lamb* is particularly favourable, as it is a symbol of the church in Christianity. Gypsy folklore says that a *ewe-lamb* is a symbol of a loyal friendship.

snake: said to represent fear or anxiety about sex, or temptation (a connotation derived from the serpent in the Garden of Eden). Some cultures, however, view the snake's ability to shed its skin and regenerate as a symbol of wisdom, so a snake dream from this point of view may be one of hope for the future.

squirrel: your subconscious may be telling you to start saving money and resources, to prepare for possible hard times ahead.

tiger: the tiger usually represents an enemy, so a dream involving one is usually a bad omen, and to escape from one is a good omen.

toad: gypsies believed that the toad was a symbol of malice, and therefore dreaming of one means that an enemy will make life very difficult for you in the near future.

tortoise, turtle: you have possibly been working too hard and not enjoying yourself enough.

walrus: according to gypsy folklore, this means that you are being lazy and wasting time.

weasel: beware of malicious people who seem like your friends.

wolf: you are either feeling lonely, or as if others are picking on

animals

you.

zoo: you feel as if your friends do not appreciate your individuality.

See also BEES, BIRDS, FEATHERS, ZOO.

anniversary a dream of any happy occasion means good times ahead.

ant(s) *see* INSECTS.

ape *see* ANIMALS.

appetite this is said to represent sexual appetite, so how it appears is important — if you're hungry or thirsty it may mean a large sexual appetite, whereas a loss of appetite has obvious meaning

applause being applauded by an audience symbolises your desire to be praised for an achievement, and is also believed to mean good luck is coming your way.

apple tree *see* TREES.

apples *see* FRUIT.

archbishop this is a bad omen meaning death, according to gypsy folklore.

argument *see* QUARREL.

arms see BODY.

arrow if you are shot by an arrow, you may feel that someone is 'out to get you' or is critical of you.

If you are trying to shoot someone with an arrow, you may wish to harm them; Freudians may say you wish a sexual relationship with that person.

ashes these are a Christian symbol of death and mourning and might mean trouble ahead.

aunt dreaming of an aunt or uncle may mean a family quarrel.

autumn if your dream takes place in autumn, it may mean that you are conscious of growing old. See also SPRING, SUMMER, WINTER.

ass *see* ANIMALS.

attack if you are the attacker you probably feel angry at a particular person or situation but are unable to do anything; attacking in a dream 'acts this out'.

If you are being attacked in a dream that is probably the way you feel in real life.

audience *see* APPLAUSE.

axe to dream of an axe symbolises death or evil in the modern world, although to earlier peoples it was the symbol of God and power.

A *pickaxe* in particular is a warning of trouble, perhaps involving fire and someone with malicious intent, according to gypsy folklore.

B

baby this is a common dream symbol. Babies need to be looked after constantly and when they appear in dreams they can represent areas of our lives. The person in the position of responsibility is important, for example:

If you are a woman and you give *birth* in a dream, this may mean simply that you desire a family; it can also mean that you have a new project or undertaking which is on your mind.

If you are worrying about looking after someone else's baby, this may represent unwelcome responsibility.

If you are a man dreaming of babies then fatherhood or other responsibilities may worry you.

A baby crying may symbolise illness.

See also CHILD.

baby animals these can represent the need to care for someone; the desire to have children; or to be looked after yourself. *See also* ANIMALS.

back to see your own back in a dream usually means bad luck or illness. It could also appear as a result of an actual back injury acting as a stimulus.

If someone has turned their back on you, you may be concerned that they are doing exactly that in real life.

bag a bag or sack is said to be a symbol for the **womb.**

bagpipes according to folklore, success and many friends are symbolised by bagpipes being played in your dream.

baldness for both men and women, dreaming about baldness can denote fears of growing old and losing youth's potency.

balloon this is a childhood object of play which symbolises a desire to be child-like and escape responsibility.

bananas *see* FRUIT.

barefoot being barefoot in a dream is said to denote success.

barley fields walking in barley fields is said by gypsies to symbolise trouble. *See also* FIELD, FARM, GRAIN, HARVEST, HAY.

bath if you are taking a bath, you may wish to rid yourself of guilt about something by 'washing it away,' or you may desire to move your life in a different direction. Traditionally, taking a bath in clean water means good luck, while the reverse is true for dirty water.

battle a battle in which you fight while dreaming probably symbolises an argument or battle on a much smaller scale.

beach dreaming of walking on a golden beach simply means that you need a holiday. if the beach is deserted, you also wish to escape crowds, and need time to think. *See also* SAND.

beacon seeing this means you will find help to solve your problems.

beads according to gypsy folklore, these symbolise wealth and success. Beads were associated with magical powers.

beans dreaming of eating these is not a good omen; illness is predicted. Dreaming of growing them is said to mean arguments.

bear *see* ANIMALS.

beard this symbolises success or personal growth, unless on a woman in which case this is a bad omen.

bed this may be a symbol of how you view your relationships with others. If you are seeking sanctuary in bed then it may be a sign that you need to retreat from work, or a stressful situation. Similarly, if being alone is the reason for going to bed, you may wish to distance yourself from a partner, or maybe they are rejecting you.

If in your dream you lie in bed to watch what is going on around you then it is likely you are not taking an active role in life.

See also CHAIR, FURNITURE.

bedroom *see* HOUSE.

bees There are several meanings associated with seeing a bee or bees in your dream.

If you are stung by a bee this is a sign of trouble ahead, possibly due to another person.

If you are, or you see, a beekeeper, this means profit.

To dream of bees working is said traditionally to mean good fortune through hard work.

Bees making honey symbolise a recent illness.

See also ANIMALS.

beetles *see* INSECTS.

behind *see* VIEWING POSITION.

bells traditionally used to ward off evil, bells nowadays are more likely to be used as alarms or warnings. If you see or hear a bell your subconscious may be trying to warn you about something, or you're worried you may forget an event in the near future.

You may also be looking forward to a celebration, e.g. a wedding.

An alarm clock ringing may enter your dream as a bell, in

which case it simply means you have to get up!

If you dream of hearing a *passing bell*, which used to be rung when a funeral passed, this means you or a member of your family will become ill.

birds these have often been considered bad omens throughout history. Dreaming of birds and other **animals** is common, as they can represent ourselves, or other people. What they represent depends on your own perception of birds, or a particular type of bird. You may be scared of birds, or admire them. It is also worth noting that some birds can talk, so if you talk to one you may be wishing to communicate with someone. As with animals, individual birds can represent different meanings:

blackbird: these birds traditionally indicate trouble and suspicion.

caged bird(s): this represents your own frustrations and resentments, or fear of being 'caged-in' yourself. If you see the bird being released this may represent a sexual freedom previously unknown.

chicken: this bird is said to represent the mother figure; if a mother dreams of a *hen* with her brood then she may be concerned for her own child(ren) leaving one day.

cockerel: this is said to represent success and power, along with the need to be vigilant (due to the cockerel's usual role). To dream of it crowing reveals that a friend may betray you.

crow: the crow represents death, and to dream of it is almost certainly a bad omen. It is said to represent, for example, a funeral or adultery.

cuckoo: this may represent someone taking from you unfairly, especially in love, or a general disappointment with a current relationship.

dove: this is a symbol of peace in dreams as well as everyday life. It represents the Holy Spirit and therefore holiness and goodness, so to dream of a dove is a good omen. It may also symbolise that you wish to personify these qualities. A *turtle dove* means that you will have a happy and faithful marriage to a kind person.

duck: according to gypsy folklore, the duck represents pleasure, success and good fortune.

eagle: not surprisingly, the eagle symbolises power and domination. It could be that you are being dominated, or you are the dominant one, using (or abusing) your power over others. Dreaming of an eagle can also mean that you will be successful in a venture and seeing one flying overhead can mean that praise will come your way soon.

falcon: according to gypsy folklore, to have a trained falcon on your arm symbolises honour.

goose: this is said to be a symbol of silliness, but geese cackling is said to mean success in business.

hawk: this is a respected and revered bird in many cultures, especially Native American. As a bird of prey, it represents skill, intelligence and insight, and to dream of one means good luck and success in business.

heron or crane: these birds are known for their voracious appetites and hunting techniques; to dream of one may denote your own aggression and wickedness.

hummingbird: this symbolises foreign travel and prosperity.

jackdaw: like the crow, this is a bad omen, although not as severe. It may mean that you will meet an enemy, according to gypsy folklore, and catching one means victory over enemies.

lark: this is a good omen of happiness, health and prosperity.

magpie: the magpie symbolises deceit and trickery, so to dream of one means someone will try to deceive you and make you unhappy.

nightingale: the nightingale is a good omen in a dream , and predicts that you will hear good news soon. According to traditional dream interpreters, if a woman who is married or in a relationship dreams of a nightingale, her children will be beautiful singers!

ostrich: this may denote your being 'cut-off' or restricted from others (due to the head-in-the-sand symbolism). it is also a sign of stupidity.

owl: this is a symbol of wisdom and knowledge, and may symbolise your need to gain knowledge in a particular area, or to ask advice from one who is wiser. Conversely, it is also said to be a symbol of sickness or death.

parrot: as the parrot is a talking bird, dreaming of one means that a secret you wish to keep may be found out, perhaps through someone eavesdropping, according to gypsy folklore.

partridge: traditional dream interpretation says that the partridge symbolises silliness and lack of intelligence. To dream of one means that you will have to deal with unintelligent or vindictive people.

peacock: this was thought to be a symbol of immortality to early Christians, but nowadays is more associated with pride and showiness. It can foretell of wealth or promotion, or it can mean that you desire more excitement in life.

pheasant: this is a very good omen in a dream. If you are carrying one it means that you will be healthy and live a successful life full of praise. If you eat a pheasant this signifies an abundance of food and other comforts; but you should not overindulge.

phoenix: this is the symbol of rebirth in waking life as well as in dreams. It means that you will gain a new lease of life and a fresh start.

pigeon: this is said to symbolise honesty and loyalty, although wild, dirty pigeons mean the opposite.

quail: this symbolises bad luck and unhappiness, according to traditional dream interpretation. The quail is also a symbol in waking life for a prostitute. If you dream of eating quails' eggs, this may mean that you have delusions of grandeur.

raven: as with the crow, this can mean trouble or adultery and is a modern day symbol of bad luck. However, some cultures thought of it as a symbol of knowledge.

robin: as the bird most associated with Christmas, this is an omen of happiness.

rook: according to gypsy folklore, this stands for efficient business.

singing birds: this symbolises joy.

sparrow: this is also a positive omen, this time representing good luck.

stork: in legend, this is the bird that 'delivers' babies, so this may be a wish-fulfilment dream.

swallow: this is a sign that things are happy at home, and that you should receive good news soon.

swan: this bird is associated with health, wealth and happiness. Its beauty and grace may be something to which you aspire, or it may represent someone with those qualities whom you admire.

turkey: this means that malicious people who try to hurt you will suffer more themselves in the long run.

vulture: this is a bad omen in a dream, and may mean that others are trying to get something from you, or attack you.

See also ANIMALS, FEATHERS.

bird's nest the symbolism here is clear: an empty nest means disappointment; a nest full of eggs means success.

birth see BABY.

birthday seeing everyone celebrate a birthday means happiness will come soon. On the other hand, if it's your birthday and everyone forgets, then you may feel you are being overlooked or not given enough attention. The people in your dream are, therefore, significant. See also CELEBRATION.

black, blue see COLOURS.

blackbird see BIRDS.

blasphemy this is a sign that you will be unhappy and plagued by bad luck. See also SWEARING.

blood see BODY.

blossom one of the first signs of spring, blossom is a fortunate symbol in a dream, indicating happiness and prosperity. See also TREES.

boat to dream of being in a small boat is said to foretell of sudden wealth. What happens to the boat can also be significant:

If the boat sails on calm, clear water, this means happiness and success will come your way.

If the sea, river, etc. is rough, or the water dirty, this means trouble ahead.

If you fall from a boat, you or someone close to you could be in danger.

Dreaming of a *gondola* means that you desire foreign travel and perhaps more romance in your life.

See also LIFEBOAT, LIGHTHOUSE, TRAVEL.

body as with **animals** and **birds,** different images from the body symbolise different feelings or parts of your character. If you dream of a healthy body, this is usually a sign of your strength or power (not just physical); it could also be wishful thinking on your part! If you dream of an unhealthy body this could mean a general worry about illness or failure. The most commonly occurring symbols are:

arms: these are a symbol of strength and also of caring and protection. If someone holds their arms out to you to protect you, it may be that you are dependent on this person in waking life, or seek reassurance from them. If you *see* arms that are weak, this is said to mean that your health or job/business may suffer; if the arms are strong, the reverse.

blood: this represents the life spirit, and if you see blood in your dream then you may fear losing spirit or strength. If an attack by another person causes you to lose blood, then your loss of strength could be caused by someone else. Blood can also represent menstruation, and a woman dreaming of blood may have health worries.

brain: this is said to symbolise illness or weakness, but you could also be worrying about your intelligence and how it is perceived.

ears: this could be a sign that you need to listen more to what others are saying. *See also* DEAFNESS.

eyes: these are a symbol of how well we deal with situations or communicate with people. If your eyes are closed, you may be avoiding the truth about a situation. If someone else's eyes are closed to you, this may mean that in waking life they are rejecting or ignoring you.

hand/finger: these symbolise creativity and communication; to lose a finger in a dream was thought by gypsies to mean bad luck. Are your hands being restricted, or do they seem healthy and strong?

head/face: these often represent the way you, or others, view yourself, e.g. as beautiful, or aloof. On the other hand, any latent feelings you have may appear in the form of a face or head which has a particular appearance or expression. For instance, an ugly, deformed face may represent ugly problems you do not wish to confront; a blank face may mean that you feel insignificant or ignored.

heart: if you dream of heart trouble, this may simply be caused by real-life physical symptoms or worries of a weak heart. If you dream of being injured in the heart, this is said to foretell of danger.

knees: if you fall on to your knees, you may be pleading for help from someone. *See also* KNEELING.

mouth: this is said to represent your desires, or possibly the female genitals. It may also be telling you to keep quiet about something, or mistrust gossips.

neck: if you dream of a strong, powerful neck this means power, praise and success in money matters. If the neck you dream of is sore or blemished, this means illness. A long, graceful neck with no lines may mean a desire to be younger or more elegant.

nose: we are said to 'sniff out' danger or 'smell a rat', and so the nose in a dream generally represents intuitive qualities. Also, a firm prominent nose can represent authority and power; a long nose can symbolise sex; a blocked nose means that you need to clear something up; and a broken nose can symbolise an argument.

penis: this represents male power and driving force, and possibly aggression.

teeth: as we bite with these, teeth symbolise aggression or, if bared, hostility. If you dream of your teeth falling out then you may be afraid of growing old or losing power. If you lose teeth it is said to mean bad luck in business, the illness of a friend or relative, or even your own death (the last interpretation is gypsy folklore). On the other hand, the dream could be due to physical stimulus, e.g. toothache or grinding your teeth.

thigh(s): you may be conscious that you are unfit and out of shape. If you dream of an injury to the thighs, you may be injured while travelling.

throat: according to folklore, if you cut someone's throat in a dream, then you may hurt them soon in waking life (but not deliberately).

vagina: this represents feminine qualities in a person, or childbearing.

wrist: you may be feeling weak and tired.

    See also GENITALS.

boil *see* ABSCESS

bones these are a symbol of death, and may be an omen, or just a representation of your fear of death.

book this is generally a fortunate symbol, denoting wisdom and knowledge. if you are learning something from the book in your dream this means you will be successful in a forthcoming venture, or changes will occur in your life for the better. if the book cannot be opened, then you may be frustrated at your lack of knowledge in a certain area, or someone is keeping a secret from you. *See also* **reading**.

boots *see* SHOES.

bottle this is a good omen which symbolises **celebrations** ahead and toasting someone's happiness. This is especially true if you dream of a wine bottle. If the bottle is broken this may mean bad luck.

bow *see* ARROW.

box this dream can have several meanings:

If you dream that you open a box to find it empty, this may mean you have been disappointed recently, or will be in the future, especially concerning money.

A box can also signify death, by representing a coffin. Note the shape and size of the box in your dream to find out whether this may be true.

If you dream of a *window box*, this is a good omen, promising a happy family life, success and longevity.

bracelet this is said to predict happiness and prosperity, in particular a good marriage.

brain *see* BODY.

brambles to dream of brambles is said to represent the desire for the unobtainable or unattainable. It is also said that the thorns represent a desire of a sexual nature.

branches to dream of branches (especially with new **leaves**) symbolises new directions and decisions, and success in business. *See also* TREES.

bread this symbolises a lack of something in your life: money, perhaps, or comfort from friends.

break dreaming of something breaking is a bad omen, and means something in your life will be broken or destroyed; the common symbols are:

arm or leg: this foretells of pain or illness. Possibly this is due to a physical stimulus which you have not yet recognised in waking life, but which your subconscious brings into your dream as a warning.

household objects: this symbolises a loss of money or property, or perhaps you simply fear this happening.

mirror: even before the 'seven years' bad luck' superstition, dreaming of a mirror was said to be a bad omen, symbolising death.

window: according to gypsy folklore, this is a warning of a fire, perhaps because the window is often the only means of escape in such circumstances. On a more general level, it may mean that you long to escape something in your life.

bride/bridegroom this may be a wish fulfilment dream, in which your subconscious expresses desires you (perhaps) did not know existed. On the other hand, men who dream of seeing themselves as bridegrooms may be expressing anxiety about a forthcoming marriage or long-term commitment.

If you see someone else (e.g. a brother, sister or friend) getting married, this may symbolise your worry that you will lose them to someone else.

See also MARRIAGE, WEDDING.

bridge dreams involving bridges are common. A bridge is a way to another area of life, a symbol of hope.

If you cross a bridge this denotes a change or new direction in life, possibly one which makes you anxious but feels right. You should note whether you could see what lies on the other side, whether anyone tried to stop you, or if there was a toll to pay. All these are significant signs which show how easy your journey is/will be.

If you burn the bridge, you are trying to separate yourself from the past, or another person. Maybe you also feel that there is no way back in a particular situation. Do you feel good or bad about this in your dream? This is also important.

If the bridge is unsteady or even broken, this symbolises a difficult road ahead with fear and possible disappointment.

If you see yourself building a bridge, this is a sign of trying to make a connection with others, or it is a possible escape route to the other side. Note whether you were anxious in your dream while building.

If you fall off the bridge, you are scared of failing in your new quest.

brook *see* STREAM.

brother *see* FAMILY.

brown *see* COLOURS.

bugle this is a good omen; the bugle is 'announcing' good news.

bull *see* ANIMALS.

bulldog *see* ANIMALS.

buoy this has an obvious symbolism: it is said to warn of danger ahead.

burglary this is a very common dream (*see* appendix), as it is something which we fear greatly in waking life. It represents a fear of losing your most cherished possessions (e.g. home, car), your privacy, or someone near to you. It could also mean that you fear losing part of yourself, such as your looks or confidence.

bus *see* TRAVEL.

butcher this symbolises illness ahead, possibly due to actual physical stimuli in the body relating to body parts the butcher is preparing.

If you are a butcher in your dream, you may be acting out aggressive feelings towards someone else.

butterfly *see* INSECTS.

C

cabbage to dream of any plant growing is a symbol of optimism, and cabbage in particular represents a long, healthy life. However, it is sometimes seen as a dull vegetable, especially by children, so to eat cabbage may symbolise that you are bored of life at present.

cage this generally represents feelings of being trapped or frustrated, sometimes sexually. If the cage door is open, you may see a way out of your present situation.

If a bird flies out of an open cage, this can represent someone leaving you, or a new personal freedom.

A bird cage already empty of birds is an omen of trouble or unhappiness.

See also BIRDS, CAPTIVITY, ENCLOSURE, IMPRISONMENT, JAILER, PRISON.

caged bird(s) *see* BIRDS.

camel *see* ANIMALS.

camera you may be looking for a hidden meaning in a situation, perhaps trying to catch someone out who you feel is lying.

candle this symbol has several interpretations:

If you dream of a lit candle, the chances are you seek spiritual enlightenment and peace; it also symbolises new life.

If the candle burns brightly, this is a good omen, denoting good health and success, maybe even marriage or a new partner.

candlestick

If the candle's flame is waning, then illness or sadness may be predicted, or maybe fears of failing health or in men, impotency.

If it remains unlit, then you may fear that you may not obtain something you desire. *See also* WAX.

candlestick traditionally said to symbolise an invitation to a wedding, the candlestick is a symbol of religion universally and so may mean you have been thinking about religious matters.

cannon dreams of weapons almost always signify aggression. It is important to note who is firing the cannon, and at whom. It is also said to be representative of the phallus. *See also* GUN, WEAPONS.

captivity this is a common and powerful dream symbol. In general, it represents your feeling of being held back, frustrated, or restricted, maybe in work or in your relationships.

It is worth noting who is holding you in captivity – perhaps someone who does not want you to break away or develop your potential? If you go along with them and do as they say, perhaps you are being too passive in real life and should stand up for yourself.

There is also a theory that the room or cell of captivity represents the reproachful mother figure, from whom we will try to break away but perhaps feel held back.

See also CAGE, CHAINS, ENCLOSURE, IMPRISONMENT, JAILER, PRISON.

car *see* TRAVEL.

cards playing cards means that you may be deceived – note with whom you are playing in your dream

carp *see* FISH.

castle this represents your need or desire for security. The more heavily defended the castle, the greater the need for security.

If you are already living in the castle, this means that you probably feel safe and secure already.

If you see yourself entering the castle, this means you are optimistic about future security (e.g. financial).

If you are trying to get in, this may mean that you need to take further measures to feel safe.

If someone is storming the castle you live in, your security may be under threat

castration this is a powerful and often disturbing dream, especially for a man. You may fear that your power or status as a man is being undermined or threatened.

If a woman dreams of castration, this may reflect feelings of hatred or rage towards a violent or over-powerful man.

cat *see* ANIMALS.

caterpillar *see* INSECTS.

cattle *see* ANIMALS.

cave the cave is the earliest dwelling-place of man and as such we feel a primeval sense of attraction to it. If you are in a cave in your dream, then the chances are that you need to escape from problems and return to basics.

Freudians also say that the cave may have associations with the warmth and darkness of the womb. It may also reflect the desire to explore the subconscious.

Nowadays you may see the 'cave' in your dream as something else: a familiar basement, a childhood bedroom, anything with the association of comfort and solitude.

celebration this means good fortune is coming your way, unless something goes wrong during the celebration. *See also* BIRTHDAY, WEDDING.

celebrities *see* FAMOUS PEOPLE.

cellar *see* HOUSE.

cemetery this may signify fear of death, or death may be on your mind due to a recent bereavement. It could also mean a desire to become more spiritual or religious.

A cemetery can also represent childhood, or people, events or a particular incident from your past. You may feel a sense of regret associated with these images.

Most dream interpreters, however, say that a cemetery symbolises a positive future too.

See also DEAD PEOPLE, DEATH, GRAVE, FUNERAL, TOMB.

chains If you are in chains, you may feel that someone is trying to hold you back, or you have a difficult problem which is weighing you down. An enemy could also try to hurt you, but you will they will not succeed in getting the better of you.

If you are chaining someone else, perhaps you fear that they will sever relations with you unless you take action.

See also CAGE, CAPTIVITY, JAILER, IMPRISONMENT, PRISON.

chair seeing yourself sitting in a chair may mean that you will take a more relaxed attitude towards life in the future, or sit back and be more objective. *See also* BED, CUPBOARD, FURNITURE.

chameleon *see* ANIMALS.

chase If you are being chased it means you are probably not facing up to a problem involving someone else, or to an aspect of your life or character which makes you uncomfortable.

If you are chasing someone else, this may mean you are trying to control them.

cherries *see* FRUIT.

chess dreaming of chess means that you like to take an

intellectual approach to life and face problems with a lot of careful thought.

If you win a game of chess, this means that you will use this approach successfully to overcome a current problem or adversary.

See also GAMES.

chicken *see* BIRDS.

child to dream of a child is said to foretell of prosperity and goodness. You may also wish a family of your own.

If you dream that you are a child, then you may wish to be protected and to avoid facing up to difficult issues.

See also BABY.

chimney *see* HOUSE.

Christ if you dream of Jesus Christ or any other benevolent biblical figure, then you are subconsciously expressing a wish to be more religious or spiritual, perhaps due to a bereavement or other trauma. *See also* GOD.

church like an **abbey**, a church is a place of reflection and peace, so dreaming of one could symbolise your need to have more calm in your life.

If you dream of going into church, *temple*, or other holy place, this may foretell of a wedding or funeral, but can also symbolise goodness and love all around you.

If you dream that you build a church, this probably means that you are very religious, or are seeking comfort in religion.

If you see a church being destroyed, this is an omen of deceit and sin.

If you are in church listening to a *service*, or if you hear church music, this symbolises that you are happy with your present religion, or spiritual beliefs.

city

See also GOD.

city a busy, bustling city is a sign of prosperity; a deserted city the reverse, according to gypsy folklore. See also VILLAGE.

clam *see* FISH.

cliff if in your dream you are standing on a cliff and looking over, afraid you will fall, then you may have a strong fear about a present situation. *See also* ABYSS, FALLING.

climbing this is a common dream (*see* appendix) symbolising our desire to 'get on' in life and tackle obstacles in order to gain praise, promotion, etc.

The climb itself is significant – how hard was the ascent? Was anyone helping or hindering you? Did you eventually make it to the top, or just keep climbing aimlessly? Ambitious people are especially likely to dream of climbing.

See also HILLS, LADDER, MOUNTAINS, VIEWING POSITION.

cloak this means you are hiding something from others. See also CLOTHES.

clock if you dream of a clock, you are probably concerned about **time**: perhaps you have little time to do something and worry you will not finish it, or maybe you are aware that you have to make the most of time at the moment. You could also be worrying about oversleeping.

Gypsy folklore says that a clock is a bad omen, but this is probably superstition, as clocks were said to stop when someone died.

closeness *see* VIEWING POSITION.

clothes these symbolise the way you present yourself to the world and your own self-image.

If you see yourself splashing out on new clothes, you would

probably like to be seen as more interesting or glamorous, or simply change people's perception of you.

If you are wrapped up in a big heavy coat or **cloak**, you may be protecting yourself from criticism or hiding something. If you see *underwear* in your dream, then this may represent sexuality.

If you are wearing familiar, comfortable clothes, you may seek comfort and protection from friends or family, or maybe you feel very secure at present due to close relationships with people.

The **colours** that you wear in your dream are also important, signifying mood, as they do in waking life. Bright colours symbolise an optimistic outlook, and dreary colours can mean that you have unpleasant feelings to deal with, or you are feeling pessimistic in general. Black may symbolise mourning.

If you take your clothes off, you probably wish you were more confident, even an exhibitionist, or would like people to see a new you.

See also NUDITY, SHIRT.

clouds The type of clouds is significant.

If the clouds are heavy and threatening, you may be feeling depressed or pessimistic, or bad luck may befall you soon.

If the clouds are light and fluffy, then this is an omen of more positive, peaceful times ahead.

Clouds can also be a symbol of **God**.

clown although these are common childhood symbols, clowns are notorious for being outwardly happy but melancholy inside. If you see a clown in your dream, perhaps you or someone you know presents a happy appearance while hiding inner sadness. If you are the clown, then you may fear looking foolish to others.

club a Christian symbol of suffering, the club represents bad luck. As a **weapon**, it is also said to have phallic symbolism.

cockerel *see* BIRDS.

colours Most of the time we dream in colour, although some people report dreaming in black and white every time. Sometimes, however, one colour will dominate. There is a general consensus as to what each colour symbolises, but the meaning may be different for you if you attach a characteristic to a particular colour. For example, you may have grown up in a bright yellow house and therefore, for you, yellow has associations of comfort and family. Keep this in mind if you dream in one prevalent colour.

black: this is the colour of darkness, death and mourning, and may symbolise sadness or depression too. Conversely, it may represent power.

blue: this is a spiritual colour and denotes calmness, tranquillity and faithfulness. If the blue is very dark, almost black, this may symbolise sadness and depression.

brown: this symbolises nature and practicality, but also dullness and depression if dark.

green: this colour is associated with nature and growth, as well as fertility and prosperity. However, it is also the colour of envy.

red: this is the colour of anger, sex and heat, as well as danger or injury.

white: symbolic of light, this colour is also associated with goodness, purity and innocence. If everything is white in your dream, this may represent heaven.

yellow: a bright, lemon yellow symbolises health and optimism, but a sickly yellow could denote illness or cowardice.

comet this is a bad omen, denoting future problems or illness.

conflict If you become involved in a conflict in your dream, this means that you have problems that you are failing to face. If the conflict ends peacefully, this symbolises your determination to resolve your problems. You may actually see the best way to do this in the dream, e.g. by confronting the person with whom you have the conflict, or by standing down and apologising

corkscrew this symbolises a friend or acquaintance who wants to know something about you.

corn this foretells of wealth, according to ancient dream interpreters.

corridor either you wish to escape a situation where you feel restricted and hemmed-in, or you are happily making a transition from one stage of life to another. A corridor is said to represent the birth canal.

courtroom *see* JUDGE.

cow *see* ANIMALS.

crab the crab is thought to be a difficult creature (hence the adjective 'crabby'); dreaming of one means you are thinking of a person you know who is difficult or bad tempered. This person may have a hard shell like the crab, and may be more pleasant underneath.

crane, heron *see* BIRDS.

cravat *see* TIE.

crescent some cultures see this as a symbol of the Virgin Mary, and it means that you will be blessed with happiness and love.

cricket *see* INSECTS.

crocodile *see* ANIMALS.

cross to see a cross means that you may be seeking guidance, particularly of a religious or spiritual nature. You may also be feeling guilty about something, or that you have made a sacrifice recently.

If you are carrying the cross, this may mean that there is trouble and suffering ahead.

cross-roads the symbolism here is obvious: you are being forced to make a choice between two or more options. There may be other visual clues as to what you must choose between, e.g. leaving home, or staying.

crow *see* BIRDS.

crowd this is generally a symbol of fun and excitement, if you are enjoying being in the crowd at a concert, for example. You will start to enjoy life more soon.

If you are anxious in the crowd and trying to get away, this represents a work situation or relationship from which you are keen to break free.

crown this is a good omen, and means that praise and honour will be rightfully yours soon. It invariably symbolises a reward.

crutches a dream of crutches may be due to an actual injury stimulating the mind to wish for a release from pain.

It may also symbolise that you need emotional support or guidance from friends or colleagues.

crying if you dream that you are crying, you may wake up feeling emotionally drained, as you would after crying in waking life. Perhaps you have dreamed of a bereaved person or someone you miss. However, dreaming of crying is often a good thing, as it allows you to 'release' in a way emotions that may have been building for some time. Moreover, crying in a dream usually means that you are now ready to get over any hurt or pain that you may have been feeling, and move on.

You should ask yourself whether the tears helped you to feel better, or whether someone deliberately made you cry, in which case you may have been hurt by that person recently and need to deal with it.

cuckoo *see* BIRDS.

cucumber this has a rather obvious association with sex; if a man dreams of a cucumber he may have performance anxiety. If a woman dreams of one she may desire a very masculine figure in her life.

cupboard a cupboard or wardrobe is said to represent the womb or a sexual image, or simply the depths of the mind. If you find something in a cupboard/wardrobe, you may be discovering something of which you were previously unaware

A locked cupboard or wardrobe means you are probably keeping a secret, or a part of you is being hidden or denied.

See also **house.**

cupid seeing the messenger of love really does mean that you will find love and happiness.

cut flowers *see* FLOWERS.

cycle *see* TRAVEL.

cypress tree *see* TREE.

D

daffodil *see* FLOWERS.

dagger like all **weapons**, this can be viewed as a phallic symbol. It can also foretell of suffering and violence.

If you are holding the dagger, however, and using it for brave deeds, then you will be successful in a future venture.

daisy *see* FLOWERS.

dancing in contemporary culture, dancing often has connotations of a sexual nature. Thus dreaming of dancing may symbolise the way that the dreamer interacts with another/others on a sexual level. If someone is dancing for you, this may indicate your desire for them, of theirs for you.

Alternatively, dancing can represent the emotional interaction of the dreamer with the rest of the world. If dancing with others, do you fit in well with their style, or are you always out of step? Perhaps you feel 'out of step' with the world in general. Maybe the music and dancing do not match, in which case you may feel that you need to examine certain aspects of your life which 'do not fit'.

dandelion *see* FLOWERS.

danger this can be a difficult dream to predict, as so much depends on your own personal interpretation, i.e. what is happening in your life at present. It is possible that your dream represents a major issue, such as a change of career, a bereavement or a worry concerning a relationship. It does not necessarily mean that you will be in danger soon, more that an important change will be, or is, taking place in your life. The key questions are: who else was in your dream? Were they helping you out of danger? Did you escape the danger, or were you stuck wondering where to turn next? Considering these may give you the answer you seek.

darkness being in darkness may mean that you are 'in the dark' about a particular issue at present, perhaps waiting for an answer or help from someone, or trying to work something out.

Darkness can also symbolise the womb, especially if you are in a *dark room* where you are warm and comfortable. This could mean that you long for security and someone to care for you.

Traditional dream interpreters also say that darkness is warning you to be on your guard against insincere friends.

deafness Dreaming that you are deaf may mean that you are unwilling to listen to what someone else has to say, or you find it hard to communicate with someone.

If someone else cannot hear what you say, then this means that you feel ignored.

See also EAR, SEEING, SMELL.

dates *see* FRUIT

day/daylight to dream of bright daylight, or day breaking, is a good omen, promising positive times ahead.

dead people if you dream of someone who is dead, but alive in your dream, there may be several reasons for this:

You may simply be missing the person, especially if they used to comfort you in times of trouble or give you advice.

There may be unresolved issues or feelings associated with that person perhaps you regret arguing with them, or not visiting them enough.

Perhaps they represent some aspect of your character, or someone else's: maybe they were too critical or worked too hard, and you worry that you may have these traits too.

deafness if you find that you are deaf in a dream, this may mean that you are not listening to people or facing up to responsibilities.

death This is a very common dream image (*see* section on TYPICAL DREAMS, p.27).

If you dream of someone else's death, it is unlikely you wish them to die. Either you are worried that they may leave you, or you wish some sort of separation from them. Often a real-life quarrel or dispute can trigger this.

If you dream of your own death, it may mean that you are worried about your own mortality or becoming ill, or you have a difficult problem on your mind, brought about by your own actions. You may also wish to be free of a particular responsibility or burden, and should think seriously about a change of direction in your life.

See also CEMETERY, FUNERAL, GRAVE, KILLING, SUICIDE.

deer *see* ANIMALS.

déja vu this phenomenon, meaning 'already seen', sometimes occurs when you see or hear something in waking life and are convinced that you have already dreamt it (the other type of déja vu occurs when you think you have had the experience previously, but in waking life). Quite often it can reveal people's knowledge about past lives. Some have dreamt of a place which they know they have not visited, then travel there to find that the place is exactly as they dreamt. No one really knows why or how it happens, but those to whom it does happen are often shocked, curious, or disbelieving.

deluge *see* FLOOD.

departure this may symbolise a real journey you will make soon, or it may also mean that you are leaving some aspect of your life behind – perhaps a relationship that is no longer working, or a job.

descent if you are descending a hill, for example, you may feel that you are failing in something. Alternatively, the descent may symbolise that a tricky problem has been conquered and you can now relax and come back down to earth.

If you descend below the ground, in a tunnel or cave for example, you may need to do some inner questioning before you can solve a current problem. *See also* CAVE, DARKNESS.

desert dreaming that you are in a desert means that you feel lonely and lost in waking life; perhaps you feel that even your friends do not understand your plight.

devil if you see the devil in your dream it is likely to mean that you have acted badly and feel guilty about it; the devil is the personification of how you feel about your actions. According to gypsy folklore, this is an unlucky dream.

dice you may feel that you are leaving too many things to chance, or to other people's whims, and you need to take control of your own fate. It could also be a sign that others may be trying to cheat you in business.

diet you may be self-conscious about some other aspect of your image, not necessarily your weight.

Seeing yourself dieting or needing to diet in a dream could also mean that you have been over-indulging in some other way and need to calm your lifestyle.

digging if you are digging for a particular thing, e.g. treasure, and find it then this means good luck is on the way. If you find nothing then the opposite is predicted.

If the soil is easy to work with and clean, this is also a omen of happiness. Dirty, lumpy soil symbolises bad luck.

See also SPADE.

dirt if you see yourself as a dirty person, this may signify a lack of self-worth. If someone else appears in your dream with dirt on them, you may feel as if they have behaved badly recently.

distance *see* VIEWING POSITION.

divorce dreaming of yourself being divorced does not usually represent exactly that; usually it means that you are anxious about a current relationship, whether business or personal. You may feel that they lack your commitment, or perhaps you wish to end the relationship.

dock this is a sign of success in business, and general prosperity.

dog *see* ANIMALS.

dolphin *see* FISH.

donkey *see* ANIMALS.

door in dreams, as in waking life, 'an open door' is held to be a symbol for opportunities available to you. You may also have to take a chance and select one door from several – this represents several options open to you. This is generally a positive dream image.

A closed door, therefore, symbolises wasted opportunities or options not available to you. Perhaps in your dream, however, you manage to open it, which means you are trying to make the best of the situation and can see a way out.

doormat if you dream of a doormat you are conscious at

present of your home and how secure it is.

If in your dream your doormat is stolen, this means that a stranger will try to some in to your house, perhaps uninvited.

dove *see* BIRDS.

dragon this dream symbol varies greatly in its interpretation. To most of us the dragon is seen as a dangerous monster, and indeed is a Christian art symbol of sin and the devil. Dreaming of one can mean you are worried about or conscious of power in some form. Perhaps you are also facing frightening problems or a dangerous person, especially if the dragon is fierce and aggressive.

The Chinese see the dragon as an intelligent being and it is represented in many of their traditional celebrations. A Chinese dragon could therefore stand for intelligence and wisdom, or perhaps celebration.

Traditional dream interpreters thought that the dragon was a symbol of global changes, especially financial ones.

Ancient Celts used the word 'dragon' to mean a leader in times of danger, and this may have been their interpretation if it appeared in a dream.

dreaming if you dream of dreaming, then it may be that you wish to be more relaxed in waking life and allow your mind to be more carefree.

You may while dreaming suddenly become conscious that what is happening is only a dream or that you have dreamt it before. This is probably because you do not like what is happening and want to reassure yourself that it's 'only a dream'. This stops your mind having to deal with any unpleasant events, as they can be dismissed as dream images.

If you dream about telling someone your dream, this means that an unusual event will happen soon, according to traditional interpreters.

drowning this is a very distressing dream which could mean that you are worried about problems which are dragging you down. It is likely that they are financial or business problems.

According to gypsy folklore, seeing yourself drowning or *sinking* in a dream may mean an illness, due to actual physical symptoms affecting your breathing and manifesting themselves in your dream.

drugs dreaming of yourself taking medicinal drugs may mean that you will become ill soon, and your body is telling you that you need medicine.

If you dream that you are taking illicit drugs, this could be a sign that you crave excitement, or that you have done something of which you should be ashamed.

If you dream that someone you know is taking illicit drugs, then it could be that you are worried about their behaviour in waking life.

drum according to gypsy folklore, this dream means trouble and arguments ahead.

Modern interpretation would suggest that you crave attention.

duck *see* BIRDS.

dust this suggests that you are concerned about a problem, but you know deep down that it will be temporary and not too serious. You could also be dreaming of a problem in the future, according to gypsy folklore, but again this will be of a temporary nature.

You may also be worried about hygiene and tidiness in your home.

E

eagle *see* BIRDS.

earth if you see the earth in your dream, this represents family, roots and what has happened in your life so far. If you have a feeling of contentedness when observing the earth, this probably means that you are happy overall with what you have achieved. If you are worried or distressed, this may mean that you wish to put right things which have gone wrong, or to try to forget the past.

Earth also represents the universal mother figure, so it could also symbolise a need to feel protected, or to look after the people and things that matter to you.

earthquake this means that you are due to go through significant changes in circumstance, and things may be difficult. This could involve broken friendships, changes in career or business, or according to gypsy folklore, bereavement. Things will settle down soon after these upheavals.

earthworm according to folklore, earthworms symbolise enemies. They may also symbolise something or someone who disgusts you.

eating this is one of our basic survival instincts, so looking or hunting for food may mean that you need to be alert in order to get through a current situation.

Eating also symbolises comfort and sharing, so if you share a meal with another this symbolises becoming closer to them; perhaps this is something you desire. Eating also satisfies a hunger, so there could be a sexual element too. Similarly, if you see yourself eating alone, this may mean that you are lonely.

The style of eating may also be significant. If you are gorging on a feast, this may symbolise excesses in your life that need to be toned down. if you are picking at your food, you may need to relax and enjoy life more.

If you see yourself eating at a **celebration**, this is a sign of good fortune.

See also FOOD, FRUIT.

echo according to traditional dream interpreters, this means that you will hear untrue news or something incredible.

It could also mean that you are fed up with the monotony of life. The symbolism of 'hearing the same things' over and over again is obvious.

eclipse a *solar eclipse* may mean that you are going to lose something dear to you. A *lunar eclipse* has a similar meaning, but this time you will not achieve something you desire.

eel *see* FISH.

eggs the egg is the symbol of new life, creation and potential.

If you dream of fresh unbroken eggs, this is generally a good dream. It symbolises your potential to do well in your career or personal life. You may also wish to have a family.

Broken or rotten eggs are the sign of trouble or a future quarrel.

See also FOOD.

eight *see* NUMBERS.

ejaculation dreaming of ejaculation is either a lustful dream about sex with a current partner, or a wish to meet someone with whom you can have a sexual relationship. In a small number of cases, ejaculation can simply represent the desire to complete a project.

electricity this is a symbol of a hidden force, perhaps your own or someone else's potential.

Dreaming of an electric shock may symbolise a recent reprimand, or guilt feelings you may have about a recent action.

elephant *see* ANIMALS.

elk *see* animals.

emerald if you give or receive an emerald, this denotes that good fortune and a blessing will come your way, perhaps in the form of money. Emeralds are also said to have strong connections with spirituality and in the past Persians used them as protection against evil.

emotions it is important to remember the emotions you were feeling while you dreamt. If you were upset, happy, jealous, etc. then you must try to remember what you were doing at the time, who else was there, which other dream symbols appeared, and so on. Your emotions can really only be analysed in the context of the whole dream.

enclosure being enclosed in your dream may represent a defensiveness you have against the rest of the world; your protection against being hurt.

It may also mean that you are being held back from doing what you want in life and are frustrated.

See also CAGE, CAPTIVITY, IMPRISONMENT, JAILER, PRISON.

enemy seeing a friend acting as an enemy means that you have concerns over their behaviour towards you, or perhaps you do not fully trust them.

entrails this is a dream symbol predicting bad luck or illness, according to gypsy folklore. It may also mean that you are concerned about your health.

equator dreaming of the equatorial region, or a similar tropical area, means good fortune and success, symbolised by the healthy climate and abundance in such an area.

ermine this is a symbol of royalty, so dreaming of ermine means that you have aspirations of grandeur or riches.

escape to escape from a situation or place is symbolic of your need to escape your present circumstances, or to forget the past. You may also wish to discover your true potential. What is important is from whom or what you are escaping in your dream: perhaps a hospital, in which case you may be putting an illness behind you; or from a workplace, which means you desire a change of career. Also, was it difficult to escape; was someone holding you back?

If something is escaping from you, this may symbolise a lost opportunity or relationship.

evening this represents a period of calm and rest after a difficult time. It can also mean that you are conscious of your old age approaching, especially if there is a sunset in your dream. *See also* NIGHT, TIME.

ewe-lamb *see* ANIMALS (SHEEP).

exams this is a common dream among students, not surprisingly, and is often accompanied by anxiety. There are several common scenarios: you arrive at the wrong exam; you have forgotten your pen; the text is written in a foreign language; you realise that you have not studied, etc. This is fear of failure manifesting itself in different ways. You may, of course, dream that you pass with flying colours, which symbolises your confidence.

This dream can also recur in adults after they have left education, and denotes stress, usually in working life (similar to that of exam pressure) as well as fear of failure.

See also SCHOOL and the section on TYPICAL DREAMS, p.27.

excrement this can symbolise your disgust at another person's actions, or towards yourself and your own behaviour.

If you dream of constipation, you may fear being seen as uptight; if you dream of incontinence, you may worry about the consequences of losing control and letting yourself go.

Traditional dream interpreters, however, thought that excrement represented wealth. Alchemists believed that they could make gold from ingredients found in faeces!

execution dreaming of your own execution means that you are probably feeling depressed with low self-esteem. Perhaps you even think that you deserve to feel this way, and are 'punishing' yourself in your dream.

exhibitionism you may wish to be more daring in real life, or perhaps you feel that you have made a fool of yourself recently. *See also* NAKEDNESS.

explosion you may be wishing for something to 'explode' in waking life – to shed inhibitions or restrictions, for example, or to release pent-up anger.

Explosive situations can also be symbolic of sexual desire, the actual explosion representing orgasm or ejaculation.

eyes *see* BODY.

F

face *see* BODY.

failure to see yourself failing in a dream is common; you are worried that you will be unable to achieve something and feel unable to admit this.

You may, on the other hand, actually realise quite rightly that something you are trying to do is impossible and cannot work, unless you think of a different approach.

See also EXAMS.

fairground according to gypsy folklore, dreaming of a fair means that you will meet people who will make you richer. Obviously this interpretation stems from the culture of gypsies, many of whom would run fairs as their business.

Another interpretation is that you wish to have more fun and make your life more interesting. Note which rides you choose to try. The *roller-coaster* may suggest that you would really like to let your hair down, whereas the big wheel may suggest a wish to see the world from a different perspective. if you go to see a FORTUNE-TELLER, then this means that you would like to be more in control of your fate.

fairy as children we believe fairies can grant wishes and look after us, so dreaming of one means that you would love to be more successful and protected. According to gypsy folklore, dreaming of a fairy means that you actually will be rich and independent, unless you are rich already, in which case you will face temptation.

falcon *see* BIRDS.

falling dreaming of falling is very common, with many people waking in a panic before they hit the ground. When the dreamer falls and lands, this is said to represent sexual intercourse.

When the dreamer is frightened that they may fall, this indicates fears of a real disaster.

A fall can also mean that the dreamer has done something wrong or let themselves down, or is heading towards an unpleasant situation. *See also* ABYSS, PRECIPICE and section on TYPICAL DREAMS (p.27).

falling leaves *see* leaves.

family your family background (or lack of it) is probably the greatest single factor influencing your life, behaviour and attitudes. Whether you grow up to be similar to your family members, or completely different due to rejecting their values, family life is significant. Also, how you relate to others usually depends on how you and your family relate to each other, e.g. the members of a very open and loving family will probably grow up to treat others in this way and perhaps be disappointed to find that other people are not always open and loving too.

If you see a particular family member in your dream, this could mean one of two things. It can mean that you have feelings connected with that person which you have to resolve, such as an ongoing power struggle or argument. It can also mean that they represent a part of you of which you may be conscious at present. For example, your sister may be kind but too naive and trusting, and perhaps you feel this is a trait that you possess too.

Generally, the appearance of a family member must be analysed in the context of the whole dream, i.e. what they were doing, how you feel about that particular person, and what emotions you were feeling in your dream.

Some family members have their own significance:

brother/sister: you may wish that you were more like your brother or sister in their behaviour, or perhaps your parents compare you to them unfavourably. It could also be that you have argued with them recently and wish to resolve this.

children: If you dream of your own children, then you may be concerned over their safety or upbringing. See also CHILD.

father: in general, fathers represent figures of authority in dreams. Perhaps you are questioning the authority of your father himself, but he may also be a symbol of a boss or official authority. This is especially true if your father is a dominant person in real life.

mother: if you dream of your mother while she is alive, this means joy and happiness, according to gypsy folklore. If your mother is no longer alive and she appears in your dream, this may mean that you are sad and in need of comfort.

See also ADOPTION.

famous people seeing famous people in your dream can be simply wish-fulfilment, e.g. kissing a good-looking film star. The person may also represent an aspect of yourself which you wish to explore, e.g. seeing a famous politician may symbolise your desire to study politics or work in a community based-job.

fan a traditional hand-held fan may be a symbol of pride over your appearance, according to gypsy folklore. It could also mean that you are shy or trying to hide some aspect of your personality. In Japan the fan is a symbol of power and authority.

farewell saying goodbye to friends means that you will change your job or move house soon.

farm if you own, or visit, a prosperous farm in your dream, this is a sign of success and good health, especially if you try, and enjoy, the produce.

If the farm is struggling, then this means bad luck in business, or poor health.

See also BARLEY FIELD, FIELD, GRAIN, HARVEST, HAY, PLOUGHING.

fat if you dream that you are becoming fat this could be a sign that you are concerned about your body (whether you feel you are too fat or too thin in real life).

Gypsy folklore suggests that dreaming of being fat is a sign of illness, possibly due to physical stimuli such as bloatedness or pressure in a particular part of the body, which you might not yet have recognised in waking life.

father *see* FAMILY.

fawn *see* ANIMALS.

fear if you feel fear while dreaming, this may give you insight into how you actually feel about a situation or person. It means that while you may seem happy and put a brave face on, or perhaps defensive and angry, you be actually be afraid. Dreams give you a chance to analyse your true feelings in this way. If you have a frightening dream, usually a nightmare, then you should note your fear as well as the images which appear, and ask why you felt frightened? Are you afraid to admit to yourself and others that you fear a particular thing or person? Or perhaps you are afraid to acknowledge a facet of your own personality, such as jealousy or meanness?

feathers these are a symbol of power. According to ancient dream interpreters, white feathers mean success, and dark feathers mean failure.

ferret *see* ANIMALS.

fever as with many dreams of **illness,** this may denote an actual physical problem, brought on by physical stimuli.

It could also symbolise ambition and extravagance which will lead to bad things happening, according to folklore.

You may also be deeply worried about some other matter and it is making you anxious and restless in the same way as a fever does, hence the obvious symbolism.

See also ILLNESS.

field if you dream of healthy, fertile fields, this is a symbol of success and prosperity. If your dream is of dry, unhealthy fields, the reverse is true. *See also* BARLEY FIELD, FARM, GRAIN, HARVEST, HAY, PLOUGHING.

fighting to fight with another in your dream symbolises a conflict with that person, although it is more likely to be of a mental or emotional nature, rather than physical. It could also mean that you are struggling to become stronger or more independent and you have to fight with conflicting ideas from others or even yourself. Emotional turmoil is almost certainly present in waking life.

figs *see* FRUIT.

finger *see* BODY.

fire this symbolises great passion in some form: e.g. love, lust or anger. It can also symbolise enlightenment and purity in some cultures.

As one of the four basic elements (fire, earth, water, air), it was believed by primitive man to have life-giving properties. But as we all know, it can be a destructive force too. It is important to note how the fire is burning – is it raging out of control, in which case you may feel threatened by a malevolent force, or is it a controlled fire which is burning things you wish destroyed or forgotten? In the latter case you may wish to move on from painful experiences or memories.

If you are unable to escape from a fire, then this may represent real fears about safety in the event of a fire, or perhaps you feel trapped by some aspect of your life.

fish these are generally believed to represent your unconscious desires or wishes (perhaps because they are underwater and somehow hidden) and they may also represent aspects of your personality that you do not yet understand. If you dream of eating fish, then, this means you are trying to discover more about these personality traits

Fish are also said to symbolise procreation, fertility and the desire for family.

In Christian symbolism, the fish can represent Jesus and the church, and is an important image throughout the Bible.

Certain fish can have particular meanings in your dream:

clam: according to gypsy folklore, to dig for clams is a good omen, meaning that you will reap rewards if you are careful with money.

carp: according to gypsy folklore, this is a symbol of good luck. The Japanese admire this fish and see it as a symbol of endurance.

dolphin: the dolphin is a creature with whom man can communicate and is held in special regard by most people as a friendly, playful creature. Even in mediaeval times it was depicted in paintings as a social creature. It is said also to help shipwrecked sailors by guiding them to safety. If you dream of a dolphin swimming this symbolises future adventures. If you see one out of water or beached, this means you may lose a friendship.

eel: this may symbolise someone you know who is 'slippery' like an eel, and is also a warning to be wary of trusting the wrong people.

lobster: this is an omen of sadness and problems, according to gypsy folklore.

oyster: this means you have to struggle and go through pain to get what you want from life. Oyster shells which are empty mean you will suffer anxiety and disappointment.

porpoise: this is a sign that you will be happy.

salmon: gypsy folklore says that the salmon represents family arguments.

shark: the shark symbolises a dangerous adversary. Even worse, if you dream that the shark eats you, then this adversary will get the better of you, according to gypsy folklore.

shellfish: if you dream of collecting shellfish, this means that you will have fun at a party soon. If the shells are full, you should be successful in future ventures. If they are empty, however, this means that you will waste time and perhaps money soon.

shrimp: this symbolises sorrow, and problems playing on your mind.

trout: this is a good omen, meaning success in money matters, especially if the trout is large.

See also CRAB, WHALE.

five *see* NUMBERS.

flames dreaming of flames is generally a good omen, denoting happiness. Flames are also a symbol in Christianity of passionate spirituality and zeal. *See also* FIRE.

flea *see* INSECTS.

fleet to see a fleet of **ships** or other **boats** means that your hopes and dreams will be fulfilled. In ancient as well as modern times, ships symbolise hope, perhaps because they deliver cargo and treasures from other lands.

floating if you see yourself floating it suggests that you are being 'carried along' by life and letting things happen to you, rather than making things happen proactively. It could also symbolise a loss of control in some area of life. See TYPICAL DREAMS, page 27.

flood if you see yourself being caught in a flood, then this may mean that you are worried about things getting too much for you, especially where business or finance is concerned. You may be experiencing losses or problems in these areas. *See also* RAIN.

flowers as with all plants, flowers are symbolic of new life and growth; a fresh start.

Flowers in a dream can also be connected with sex. It is said that the flower in full bloom represents the sexually active female, while a bud may symbolise the male or female genitals. If you see full, vibrant flowers, then this means that sex is on your mind in some form or another. If flowers are destroyed in your dream, then this may point to your feelings being hurt in connection with sex.

Certain flowers and images of flowers in dreams also have universally acknowledged symbolism:

acacia flowers: according to gypsy folklore, this is a symbol of inner peace and rest. According to ancient Egyptians, this flower represented woman; perhaps one known to you.

cut flowers: these represent death or illness.

daisy: this is a symbol of the sun, and can represent love and fidelity. If you dream of daisies in an unhappy context, however, you may be unsure of your feelings of love towards someone.

daffodil: the symbol of springtime, this flower is said to foretell of good news and health.

dandelion: although not an unattractive flower, the dandelion is regarded as a weed or pest to gardeners. Hence to dream of one means that someone will try to annoy or hurt you.

hyacinth: this is said to predict wealth or success.

lily: this flower is often associated with mourning, but in a dream it can symbolise purity and innocence, as well as birth, regeneration and the afterlife. A happy life through goodness and kindness is predicted. In particular, *tiger lilies* are said to represent money; *Lily of the valley* represents humility; the *lotus* symbolises immortality.

marigold: this flower, called 'the flower of light', is a good omen in a dream, denoting a faithful, happy marriage, and prosperity with wealth. It was known in earlier centuries for saving people who had been enchanted by magic.

orchid: this is a symbol of love and romance, and rare treasures.

pansy: this is a well-known symbol in waking life of kindness and goodness, of remembering others. In a dream it represents someone you love, but it may also mean that you will not be well-off.

poppy: according to gypsy folklore, this flower means you may become ill, or you may hear soon that someone you know is ill. The interpretation here stems from the fact that the poppy is used in the manufacture of opium and heroin.

primrose: this is a bad omen, foretelling of unhappiness and illness, even death.

rose: red roses are an obvious symbol of love, and white roses mean purity. Black roses symbolise death and mourning. Roses of no specific colour are generally an omen of happiness, unless wilted, in which case problems are predicted.

spring flowers: these foretell of joy.

thistle: in general the thistle represents minor annoyances, especially if you prick yourself on one in your dream. If you dream of cutting down thistles, this represents an exchange of angry words.

violet: in general these are a sign of success. If you see more than one violet, out of season, you will experience extremes of emotions, good or bad.

See also TREES.

fly *see* INSECTS.

flying it is very common to dream that you are flying and surveying all beneath you. This can suggest that you would like to see more of the world, or that you need to see it from a different perspective. It is generally a dream accompanied by feelings of happiness.

You may also wish to be free of restrictions and frustrations. It could be that your job, family, partner or lack of money are responsible for holding you back and you would like to be more independent and free.

Some interpreters say that people suffering from vertigo often dream of flying, perhaps as a way of facing fears about heights.

Flying can also symbolise a desire to be more sexually adventurous.

See also TYPICAL DREAMS, page 27.

fog this is a dream symbolising uncertainty, according to gypsy folklore. It suggests that you need to look more closely at a business matter, or to be more perceptive in waking life. You perhaps feel a little lost at present.

food this represents our survival and health. We are nourished by food and so dreaming of tasty things to eat suggests a desire for nourishment and comfort.

To share food with another symbolises your desire for a closer relationship with them, perhaps of a sexual nature, perhaps just friendship.

Having too much food suggests extravagance, and may be a prediction of illness.

Fresh food can denote a desire to start afresh with your life.

See also EATING, FRUIT.

foreign countries *see* TRAVEL.

forest according to traditional interpretation, a forest is an omen of bad luck and extreme sadness. This is due to ancient beliefs that bad spirits such as witches and goblins lurked in forests. Nowadays it is believed that a forest represents secrets or mystery. They can be peaceful or dangerous places, depending on how you feel when you are in the forest.

If you are hiding in a forest this symbolises a secret or some hidden guilt.

If you have lost your way and feel frightened, this represents a fear of not knowing which path to take in life.

If there are few healthy plants and many dead leaves, this suggests that a current friendship or relationship is unsatisfactory.

See also TREES.

forge a blacksmith's forge means that you will be successful in a future venture, but only through much hard work.

fortune-teller if you consult a fortune-teller in a dream this may mean that you wish to be more in control of your fate, by knowing what is going to happen in advance and being prepared for it.

According to gypsy folklore, it can be a prediction that you will be deceived by people you know soon.

If you dream of being a fortune-teller, this can mean that you consider yourself an authority on others' lives, and may be interfering. On the other hand, maybe you do have psychic qualities and your subconscious is using this image to tell you. Note what it is that you are predicting in the dream and whether it comes true.

fountain the fountain is the symbol of life, youth and healing, especially in a religious context. If the fountain in your dream has clear, clean water this means that if you are unwell, you should recover soon, and if you are healthy then you should prosper. *See also* WATER.

four *see* NUMBERS.

fox *see* ANIMALS.

fratricide this is a very unpleasant dream to experience, and while it usually does not mean that you actually wish to harm your sibling, you may have pent-up hostilities about someone close to you. if you have this dream it means you may fail in a future venture.

frog *see* ANIMALS.

(in) front *see* VIEWING POSITION.

frost this could mean that a love or friendship has come to an end rather suddenly. To someone in business, it can also mean that you will have difficulties soon. See also ice.

fruit all fruit is associated with health, life and/or sex. The ripening process has obvious links with sexual maturity or otherwise. Specific fruits have their own symbolism:

apples: in gypsy folklore, apples are associated with youth, whereas in Christianity they are symbolic of yielding to temptation and sin. Ripe apples are a good omen for love and business; unripe apples mean the opposite. Many, especially Freudians, say the apple is a symbol of eroticism.

bananas: these are said to symbolise misfortune, according to gypsies.

cherries: dreaming of these represents fertility and good health, and eating them denotes love. However, if you gather them, it is said to mean deception by a woman.

dates: these symbolise strong admirers or enemies.

figs: in general, seeing figs is a sign of happiness. The Ancient Romans felt they were a symbol of life and success. However, eating figs may mean bad luck financially, but a strong marriage, according to gypsy folklore.

gooseberries: these are ancient symbols of fertility so to dream of them means your plans will be fruitful or you will have a large family.

grapes: grapes also symbolise fertility and happiness, so any plans made should work well. *Vines* also represent fertility and prosperity, especially if you pick the grapes.

melon: dreaming of melon is said to mean recovery after an illness. According to gypsy folklore, the plentiful juice helped to dispel a fever.

fruit

olives: these denote peace and happiness; your present circumstances should improve.

oranges: dreaming of eating oranges is traditionally said to represent anxiety and problems

peaches: according to Chinese tradition, these are a symbol of a long happy life.

pears: these are said to represent sickness.

pineapples: gypsy folklore states that pineapples mean good health and prosperity, and a feast in the future.

plums: if the plums in your dream are ripe, this is a good omen. If they are unripe, this may predict illness. If they are rotten, your friends may betray you and money troubles are likely.

prunes: this is an omen of good health and happiness, according to gypsy folklore.

pumpkin: this means that you have admirers that you may not know about. However, according to gypsy folklore, if you dream of eating a pumpkin you may be ill soon.

raspberries: traditional dream interpretation suggests that eating raspberries in a dream means sadness and regrets.

strawberries: dreaming of these means good luck.

watermelon: according to gypsy folklore, a watermelon is a sign of illness.

See also EATING, FOOD, TREES.

funeral Dreaming of your own funeral is common, especially among adolescents, who often imagine this scenario in waking life. You probably seek reassurance that you will be missed, and that people will say good things about you.

Seeing the funeral of someone who has recently died is

usually your subconscious trying to deal with the loss.

Traditionally, it was said that dreaming of the funeral of a relative meant a happy marriage and prosperous times ahead!

Attending a *wake* in your dream means that you may be unwilling to accept that the bereaved person has really gone from your life.

See also CEMETERY, DEAD PEOPLE, DEATH, GRAVE.

furniture this represents all that you have built up or achieved over the years, as well as problems or issues that you may not have dealt with fully. It can also represent how well you cope with life. If you see a room with a lot of clutter and/or worthless items, you may need to confront problems from the past, or simplify your current lifestyle. If the room is sparsely furnished and uninviting, it may be that you do not let enough friends or warmth into your life, or are seen as aloof. *See also* BED, CHAIR, CUPBOARD, TABLE, WARDROBE.

future dreams of the future fall into two types:

You may dream about how you would like the future to be, e.g. meeting a wonderful partner, having a successful business, and so on. This is simply wish-fulfilment and your dream may or may not come true.

You may also dream about events which do actually come true, and which you had no feasible way of predicting. Why this happens is not fully understood but it may be that your psychic powers are strong and you actually can predict the future in your dreams. Another reason may be that you are very close to a particular person and you have correctly guessed that something will happen to them (e.g. a careless driver will have an accident). However, this does not fully explain why some people can dream of plane crashes, for example, or natural disasters, before they happen. Cynics will always say that this is coincidence. One thing is certain: those to whom it has happened believe it. *See also* DÉJA VU.

G

gallows if in your dream you are hung on the gallows, this could mean that you have done something bad for which you should be punished.

Surprisingly, gypsies saw this as a symbol of success, the height of the gallows being directly proportional to the height of success you will reach.

gambling *see* GAMES.

games These can represent a desire to be more playful or carefree. Alternatively, your game-playing strategy can symbolise your approach to life. Are you competitive and aggressive, do you play fairly, or do you stand on the sidelines while others do all the work?

If you are *gambling*, this may be a sign that you are taking too many risks in life.

See also CHESS.

garden the garden can symbolise how you view your life, and also your inner feelings and potential for growth.

A tidy, well-kept garden means you are likely to be an efficient and organised person; perhaps too controlled or inhibited?

An unruly garden suggests that you need to take more control over your life and become more organised. You may not pay enough heed to your health, work or relationships, and you could also lack direction.

A beautiful or exotic garden suggests that you are happy and contented at present.

Attractive gardens are also said to be omens of future happiness, while untidy gardens may mean trouble ahead, but nothing that cannot be solved.

Gardens may also be simple settings for our dreams, which may symbolise a desire either simply to have a garden, or to be among nature.

gardener people who tend the land are generally a good omen, according to gypsy symbolism. A gardener means good luck and prosperity.

garland this symbolises happiness and glory.

gate going through a gate is said to symbolise a deeper level of inner understanding. It represents a desire to increase self-knowledge. It may also mean that you are seeking the answer to a question or the solution to a problem.

Going through the gate may also represent achieving something which you previously thought was impossible. It is worth noting what lies beyond the gate to gain a clue about what this something is: a new job, a course of learning, etc.

If someone goes through the gate with you, this means either that they want to help you with your quest for inner knowledge, or that your relationship with them is moving to a new level.

gems dreaming of gems means that you will go up in the world, according to gypsy folklore. *See also* EMERALD, JEWELLERY.

genitals these often represent parts of our sexual personality; for example, if you are a man and you dream that you have the genitals of a woman, then you could be conscious of the feminine side of your nature in relation to sex.

ghosts ghosts may represent yourself (perhaps you feel ignored or undervalued), or memories of the past which torment you.

They can also represent a guilty secret which keeps 'haunting' you.

If the ghost is of a bereaved person you know, then this either symbolises the loss you feel following their death, or the fact that their attitudes and beliefs still influence you. As you start to get over the grief this sort of dream should occur less.

giant this is a common dream symbol for children, as they appear in story books frequently as mystical figures. Perhaps the child has recently been reading about giants and is afraid. Alternatively, giants can simply represent adults in authority such as parents or teachers.

If you dream of a giant as an adult, this may be due to a deep-seated fear which you experienced as a child. It could also be a new fear but one which manifests itself in the shape of a familiar childhood figure.

See also MONSTER, OGRE.

gifts these rarely represent actual gifts in the material sense; more probably it is gifts of an emotional or spiritual nature that are being symbolised. Perhaps you have done a good deed recently for someone and they were very grateful – you may see this in your dream as an exchange of gifts.

The 'gift' could also be something bad that you have done to another person, or they to you, in which case the gift in the dream could be distorted, offensive, or just an empty box.

See also PRESENT.

glasses *see* SPECTACLES.

goat *see* ANIMALS.

God if you dream of seeing or meeting God, it does not

necessarily mean that you have a new religious calling or wish to become more spiritual. This can, of course, be the reason, and you are maybe assessing your religious beliefs and thinking about life and death. maybe you feel that you have not attended CHURCH as often as you would like, or there is a service such as a WEDDING to look forward to.

Alternatively, God can represent any authority figure such as a parent or boss, and this suggests that you desire someone else to help with a present situation or problem. It could also mean that you are conscious that you do not hold all the power in your relationships and others play an important part.

God can also appear as an omniscient figure, chastising you for something. This may be your own guilt over your behaviour or actions, or a fear of being found out, or a reminder that you must take responsibility for what you have done.

See also RELIGION.

gold this usually represents that which you hold dear to you, not necessarily gold or money.

If you dream of having lots of gold in your pocket or purse, this means the opposite will be true. if you come across gold and silver and pick it up then you will lose money and be lied to by friends.

If the gold is tarnished, or if it is 'fools' gold', then the values you hold dear are unworthy and should be rethought. Perhaps you are too materialistic or selfish.

If you dream of wearing golden garments, this is a sign of happiness and praise. If you are wearing a gold crown, then you will be highly praised by those in authority, but beware you do not become big-headed.

gondola *see* BOAT.

goose *see* BIRDS.

gooseberries *see* FRUIT

gore seeing gore or blood from an accident or fight is said to be an omen of terrible trouble. See also BODY.

grain like a dream of a prosperous FARM, a dream of grain in plentiful supply is a good omen, symbolising success and abundance. Seeing a healthy field of grain means profit and harvesting this grain means enjoying the benefits of the profit.

If you see yourself wearily carrying the grain, or if the harvest is poor, then life will be tiring and hard in the near future.

See also BARLEY FIELD, FIELD, HARVEST, HAY, PLOUGHING.

grapes *see* FRUIT.

grass if you are walking through grass this is a good omen, denoting happiness and success, especially if the grass is lush and healthy.

If you see grass which is withered and brown, then this is a sign of bad luck and maybe sickness.

If you eat grass then this is also a bad sign, probably of sickness.

See also FIELD, GRAIN.

grasshopper *see* INSECTS.

grave Seeing a grave may be your way of coming to terms with your mortality.

If you see your own grave, it symbolises a difficult problem you are dealing with, or some aspect of your life that is now over and 'buried'.

If you see a body being carried to a grave, covered in a *pall*, this has a contrary meaning: that you will go to a wedding soon.

See also CEMETERY, DEAD PEOPLE, DEATH, FUNERAL, TOMB.

green *see* COLOURS.

grindstone this is a symbol of future success, but only through hard work and dedication.

ground being on the ground or falling to the ground represents embarrassment or humiliation.

guard *see* SENTRY.

guilt like many emotions that we feel in dreams, guilt has to be examined in the context of the whole dream. Perhaps you feel guilty about your actions or behaviour, or maybe a parent or friend is trying to control you using guilt. Who else appears in the dream? Do you stand up to them, or realise that they are right and apologise? These questions may help to analyse guilt feelings in waking life.

guitar dreams of MUSIC are generally happy ones, and the guitar is a positive symbol, denoting good luck and happiness.

gun like the CANNON and all other WEAPONS, the gun is a symbol of aggression and hostility and may symbolise your worries about these traits in yourself or others.

It is also said to represent the phallus, and may mean that you are anxious about sexual performance.

According to gypsy folklore, to hear the sound of a gun being fired may mean that you are concerned about having bad things said of you. If the gun you dream of is a *pistol*, this symbolises attacks from enemies.

gypsies dreaming that you are a gypsy, or have run away to join a gypsy family, may symbolise a desire for freedom and independence. It could also mean that you are interested in the romantic myths and legends surrounding gypsies.

H

hail this is a dream foretelling of trouble and sadness. If there is thunder or storms in your dream too, this predicts illness. One strange meaning, according to traditional dream interpreters, is that the poor will be protected as they are at peace during storms!

hair hair represents our status in life and how we view freedom and independence. Types and colours can have particular significance:

dark, short hair: this is believed to symbolise bad luck.

hair falling out: this may mean that you are insecure about your appearance, especially if you are normally worried about ageing. If you are a woman and you are bald in your dream this is said to predict a loss of money or hard times in general. If you are a man who is bald in his dream, this may also be the case in waking life and your dream reflects real feelings about it. If you dream that your hair is thinning slightly, this symbolises poverty. However, the gypsy interpretation is that anyone seeing a bald man in their dreams is due to receive riches and good health.

long hair: if you dream of having long, free-flowing hair then this signifies a yearning for more freedom. If you are a man and you dream of having long, glossy hair, this may mean that you are conscious of a feminine side to your nature; you may even be worried about being perceived as effeminate. If your hair is darker than usual as well as longer, this is said to mean that you will become richer.

tangled hair: this denotes problems or arguments which you may lose, or be losing, at present. There is possibly a legal element to the argument.

white hair: this represents dignity in old age, and honour. However, if you see you hair suddenly turning white in a dream, this means you may lose money soon.

hammer this may mean that you feel under attack at present, or that you are being held back by someone.

hand *see* BODY.

hanging to see yourself being hanged may mean that you feel guilty about something and feel you should be punished.

The opposite interpretation, favoured by gypsies and the Ancient Egyptians and Persians, is that success will come to you if you are being hanged in a dream. It was believed to mean success and wealth. By the same token, if you are about to be hanged and you are rescued or spared, then this means bad luck and loss of money!

If you sentence someone else to be hanged, you may be angry with that person in waking life (although you almost certainly do not wish that fate on them). You may also feel that you have been too harsh with them and your subconscious is trying to shock you into realising this.

hare *see* ANIMALS.

harem or hareem according to gypsy folklore, dreaming of a harem means in waking life you are being lazy and weak.

If a man dreams of a harem, this could also be wish-fulfilment or a desire for SEX without commitment.

harvest to bring in a plentiful harvest means prosperity. Harvesters, like GARDENERS, symbolise success through hard work. if you dream of them doing nothing then times may be hard. *See also* BARLEY FIELD, FARM, FIELD, GRAIN, HAY, PLOUGHING.

hatchet this is a bad omen, predicting danger or even a bereavement.

hawk *see* BIRDS.

hawthorn this means a loyal friend or lover.

hay like any dream of GRAIN this symbolises that you will reap the rewards of hard work, and live prosperously. *See also* BARLEY FIELD, FARM, FIELD, HARVEST.

head *see* BODY.

headache this may actually mean ILLNESS, or that you will wake up with a headache; the physical stimuli is the obvious reason here. It can also mean trouble ahead, even a loss of money.

health if you dream of being in good health, this is a sign that you feel strong and powerful, mentally or physically. If you dream that you are unhealthy, you could be ill, or perhaps just concerned about your health.

heart *see* BODY.

heat this symbolises passion, whether lustful, or romantic, or perhaps even angry passion. The context is important here: who else is in the dream, whether you are arguing with another, or attracted to someone you know.

There may also be a physical stimuli which makes you feel hot (e.g. an electric blanket left on).

heather this plant predicts a good future full of hope, unless it is withered or dead, in which case your hopes may be dashed.

heaven to dream that you are in heaven does not mean that you are going to die; it may mean that you will be praised and honoured soon.

You may also dream of heaven if you wish to be reunited with a recently bereaved person.

Heaven may also represent a new start and new environment that you are longing for, somewhere more peaceful or trouble-free than your current environment. Perhaps you are having trouble at work or do not like where you live?

See also GOD, HELL.

hedgehog *see* **animals.**

hedges if the hedge is thorny or prickly, this symbolises trouble and difficulty. Freud may have ascribed a fear of sex or intimacy to the symbolism of the thorns.

If the hedge is green and pleasant, then prosperous times are ahead.

height *see* VIEWING POSITION.

hell dreaming that you are in hell may predict illness or great unhappiness, or it may mean that you need to escape your present environment. *See also* GOD, HEAVEN.

hen *see* **birds.**

herbs if you dream of herbs used in cooking or healing this is a good omen denoting health and happiness. Dreaming of these fragrant herbs may also be due to a pleasant smell you are aware of during sleep.

If you dream of poisonous herbs, however, you may be in danger in the near future, according to gypsy folklore.

herd of cattle *see* ANIMALS.

herdsman a cattle herdsman is a sign of future prosperity, especially to those with little money. If you are wealthy, however, it may mean that someone will try to take your money away soon.

If the herdsman is a *shepherd*, this symbolises Jesus, or simply goodness, charity and a humble life.

hermaphrodite to dream of an person, animal, plant with male and female characteristics may symbolise a desire to explore your sexuality, or an inner struggle concerning sex. Perhaps you are hiding something that you feel may be taboo.

It may not relate to sex at all but actually symbolise a choice you have to make.

hermit *see* PRIEST.

heron, crane *see* BIRDS.

hiding if you are the one hiding in your dream, this may mean that you have a secret to hide, or perhaps you are afraid to reveal some aspect of your personality. You may also have feelings for another person which you wish to reveal but cannot.

If you are afraid while hiding that you will be discovered, this usually mean that you hide your emotions for fear of being ridiculed.

hills hills often represent a challenge you are facing. If you climb the hill, this is indicative of an uphill struggle to achieve your goals. Ambitious people often dream of hills that they have to climb to reap some reward. If you reach the top then you should overcome your obstacles and be successful. If you dream that you keep climbing and never reach the top (especially in recurring dreams) this means your ambition may never be realised.

If you are going downhill quickly and find your speed

increasing all the time, this means a loss of control over your life. Note whether you stop with a crash, or manage to slow yourself down (which means you are determined to take control again).

Lush green hills are said to represent the female body, in particular the breasts and stomach, and can therefore have a sexual connotation. They can also symbolise hope if seen from a distance.

See also CLIMBING, MOUNTAINS, VIEWING POSITION.

hog *see* ANIMALS.

holly this is a good omen, according to gypsy folklore. It symbolises happiness.

holes these may represent the womb or vagina. If you see yourself appearing out of a hole this may symbolise the birth process, whereas entering a hole can either symbolise the desire for sexual intercourse or for a return to the safety of the womb.

You may also wish to hide away from something frightening: see HIDING.

Holes are also said to represent the subconscious mind, undiscovered knowledge, or even death.

It is important to note the context in which the holes appear – if they offered sanctuary (the WOMB), if their presence scared you (DEATH), and so on.

home the home is usually a symbol of safety and comfort. Of course, if your real-life home was not a safe, comfortable place, then dreaming of home may mean that you are afraid of something, or wish to block out the past.

homosexuality if you dream of being in a homosexual relationship, one interpretation is that this is a true reflection of your sexuality that has previously been hidden.

However, in most cases it symbolises a desire to explore our own sexuality, whether homosexual or heterosexual, and maybe to find a new partner.

It can also be simply the desire for more love and affection, from either sex. This does not necessarily mean sexual or romantic love, but love from family and friends.

See also SEX.

honey according to traditional interpreters, this is a good omen, promising success. The symbolism is taken from the 'land of milk and honey' spoken of in the Bible.

hops the flowers of the hop plant give their taste to beer and have a soothing quality, so dreaming of hops is a sign of calmness and prosperity.

hornet *see* INSECTS.

horns these are a symbol of power in animals, and to dream that you are wearing horns means that you wish for power, fame and fortune. Psychoanalysts such as Freud saw horns as having phallic symbolism.

horror if you feel horror or FEAR in a dream, this means that you have a genuine horror of something in real life, but your dream will probably exaggerate the situation in order to make you confront whatever is troubling you. Like any EMOTION in a dream, this should be examined in the context of what is happening in the dream, who else is there, etc.

horse *see* ANIMALS.

horse chestnut the unpeeled horse chestnut, or conker, is said to denote arguments and worries, perhaps because of the prickly outer shell.

horseshoe this is well-known symbol of good luck, and in a dream means that you will be successful in business and relationships.

hospital this is a warning symbol; you are probably working too hard and need to relax more. You may also be worried about your health.

See also FEVER, JAUNDICE, ILLNESS

hounds see ANIMALS (DOG).

house the house is a symbol of yourself and the parts of the house represent different feelings or parts of your character.

If you see yourself building a house then this is a good omen for a future project.

If you are in a strange house then you are probably undergoing a big change in your life, or contemplating one.

If you are stuck in a house with no escape, you may be feeling 'stuck' in life too.

Ask yourself how you feel in the room you dream about. It may be that a need or desire relating to the room is being fulfilled, or you wish it to be. The parts of the house you see are significant:

bedroom: this is a place to escape to and feel safe, or a place associated with sex.

cellar: gypsy folklore suggests that a cellar foretells of sickness. It may, however, suggest that you want to retreat somewhere familiar and quiet. See also cave.

chimney: a lit chimney is a sign of prosperity and financial security in the home.

kitchen: often the heart of the house and a place where you are fed, so it symbolises the desire to have your emotional needs met.

roof: according to gypsy folklore, dreaming of the roof is a symbol of your authority and grace.

walls: these keep you warm and protected from danger.

    See also FURNITURE.

howling if you hear howling in your dream, this is said to foretell of death, according to gypsy folklore. There may not be any basis in this other than superstition surrounding howling. It may also mean that you are going through an emotional turmoil at present and the howling represents your feelings.

hummingbird *see* BIRDS.

hunger you may be lacking emotional or spiritual support at present. *See also* STARVATION, THIRST.

husband dreaming of your husband or *wife* means that you are conscious of your love for them, or are concerned about their health or behaviour.

hyacinth *see* FLOWERS.

hyena *see* ANIMALS.

I

ice not surprisingly, this is a symbol of coldness, whether emotional or physical. It could be that you or your partner have suffered a loss of libido. Maybe a relationship has come to an end and you are shutting someone out or vice versa.

It could also mean that your body has become cold while sleeping.

If you are a young woman and you dream of *icicles* this means you will marry an older man, according to gypsy folklore.

See also FROST.

idiot if you dream that you are an idiot, then you may have a problem with your self-image, and feel that people do not take you seriously.

According to traditional interpretation, dreaming of being an idiot means that you will be successful and praised wherever you go.

illness if you dream that you are ill, then there is likely to be a problem in waking life. This could mean that something is physically wrong, and your subconscious knows this. Alternatively, you could be stressed or under pressure and your dream is trying to tell you this by showing you what might happen if you do not slow down. It could also mean that you are feeling guilty or depressed about something in the past, and your feelings have now come to a head.

illumination

If you dream that you are being cared for by another person, this may point to a desire for more attention or protection from those around you in waking life.

If you are the 'carer' for someone else who is ill, this may mean that you are confused about your feelings towards that person. What happens in the dream is important: do you like the fact that they are dependent on you; or are you neglecting them, feeling that they are too needy?

See also FEVER, HOSPITAL, JAUNDICE.

illumination *see* LIGHT.

imprisonment if you are imprisoned in your dream, you are probably feeling that something is holding you back or frustrating your ambitions. What this is can vary: family problems, a partner restricting your freedom, lack of promotion at work, and so on. Perhaps you are the one holding yourself back because you fear failure or change.

See also CAGE, CHAINS, CAPTIVITY, ENCLOSURE, JAILER, PRISON.

imp according to gypsy folklore, the imp is a mischievous, even malicious, creature, so dreaming of one means you will be deceived or disappointed.

incense this is a dream of false flatterers and people trying to cheat you. It could also be something you smell while asleep manifesting itself in your dream.

infection the infection you dream of is unlikely to be a real one; it is probably symbolic of a problem you have which is playing heavily on your mind. It may be just a trivial matter, but could be an ongoing problem which will not go away without serious attention. it is likely that it is of a personal rather than business nature.

See also ABSCESS.

infirmity if you see yourself becoming old and infirm, this can reflect an actual weakness in the body that concerns you. On the other hand you may just be worrying about growing old.

insects, spiders, etc dreaming of insects and other small 'creepy crawlies' can mean several things. They may represent small, irritating problems. If you feel disgust at seeing insects, this may relate to feelings of disgust at something else, such as sex.

If you are a mother and you dream of insects flying away, this may represent fears or other feelings relating to your children leaving home.

According to traditional dream interpreters, insects symbolise loss or health problems.

Certain insects have their own particular significance:

ants: this dream may mean success for a hard-working person, or maybe just hard work!

beetles: if you see many beetles and feel disgusted, you may be overwhelmed by feelings of distaste elsewhere in life, e.g. relating to sex.

butterfly: this represents playfulness and fickleness; possibly a more carefree side of your own nature. According to gypsy folklore, the butterfly symbolises a lack of thought and purpose – maybe this is also how you behave, or how others see you.

caterpillar: this is a symbol of someone or something trying to destroy your happiness, an interpretation brought about by the way caterpillars can destroy crops.

cricket: this is said to be a good omen, meaning that you will meet up with old friends.

flea: you could dream of being bitten by fleas because you are uncomfortable or itchy in bed. It could also be that something minor is irritating you in real life.

fly: this symbolises an annoying person who may try to destroy your reputation.

grasshopper: this is a symbol of unwise decisions and bad luck, according to traditional interpreters. Dreaming of one means that you will lose money or remain poor due to laziness or bad decisions.

hornet: this represents small and trivial annoyances.

locust: this is a symbol warning you not to spend beyond your means, or any happiness will be temporary, and misery will swiftly follow.

maggot: this insect can symbolise illness or physical pain, or maybe an emotional problem.

mosquito: according to gypsy folklore, this foretells of enemies annoying you with trivialities.

moth: dreaming of a moth symbolises a relationship in which you are hurt or betrayed, according to gypsy folklore. This interpretation may stem from the familiar image of the moth being hurt by a flame.

scorpion: the scorpion is a symbol of war or arguments, and is famous for its sting in the tail. Dreaming of one is a warning of enemies who seem like your friends.

snail: a snail is a sign that you will be rewarded for your hard work with an advancement. However, if the snail's horns are an important feature of the dream, this symbolises promiscuity and/or unfaithfulness.

spider: in general, the spider is an omen of success in money matters. If you dream of a spider spinning its web in front of you, this means that you will have an abundance of money. It also stands for intelligence and great planning, so you or someone close to you will display these qualities. However, if you dream of dusty cobwebs in a room, this foretells of illness.

sting: a sting by an insect warns of a malicious person trying to harm you.

wasp: this represents a jealous person who means to harm you.

worms: these can symbolise problems which are 'eating away' at you, or a tricky relationship.

See also BEES.

invisibility if you dream of an invisible force, this may represent a force or authority stronger than you, and one which may be threatening to you.

If you are invisible to everyone else, then you are feeling neglected and ignored in waking life.

iron this metal is not a good omen. If you are hurt with, say, an iron bar, this means you or your property will suffer losses. If you dream of being a scrap merchant dealing in iron, then you may be unlucky in business and lose money.

island dreaming of an island suggests loneliness and isolation. Perhaps you are presently feeling lonely and 'cut-off' from those around you. According to gypsy folklore, isolation is actually predicted by this dream.

On the other hand, you may actually wish to escape to a peaceful place and be alone.

The other possibility is that an island, especially a calm, tropical one, represents the foetus floating in the amniotic fluid (the sea).

ivory this is a dream predicting prosperity and wealth.

ivy this is a good omen, denoting strong, loyal friendship. The ivy is a symbol of the Holy Trinity.

J

jackdaw *see* BIRDS.

jailer if you dream that you are in prison, this signifies restrictions on your independence and freedom. The jailer, then, is the symbol of what or who is holding you back. it may be someone you know, in which case they may be the ones imposing restrictions on you. Or it may be an unknown face, which could mean that a 'faceless authority' is stopping you from progressing, e.g. work.

You could also be the jailer as well as the prisoner, in which case your own fears may be stopping you from moving on in life.

See also CAGE, CAPTIVITY, CHAINS, ENCLOSURE, IMPRISONMENT, PRISON.

jasmine this is a good omen; a symbol of sincere romantic love and prosperity.

jaundice – this is said to predict actual illness or a loss of money.

jewels if you dream of jewels or jewellery, this does not necessarily mean money or material goods. They stand for anything of value or importance. Hence jewels could represent family, freedom, love friendship or wealth.

If you find jewels or *treasure* this is an omen of prosperity, according to gypsy folklore. This has connections with fairy stories in which characters find treasure as a reward for good deeds.

If someone is wearing flashy or fake jewellery in your dream, their motives may not be pure.

See also EMERALDS, GEMS.

journey *see* TRAVEL

judge a judge, *jury* or *courtroom* can symbolise your own conscience chastising you for wrong-doings.

Judges can also represent figures of authority or power, or perhaps someone whose opinion you respect.

According to gypsy folklore, appearing before a judge can symbolise wrongful persecution against you. This may be stem from the fact that gypsies often feel persecuted by the legal system and authorities.

If *justice* is upheld and you are treated fairly, this is a good omen.

jump if you jump successfully from one place to another in your dream, this represents a change or step forward that you have taken, or should take in the near future.

If you jump and fail to land successfully, this means your venture may fail, or you have just made an error of judgement.

jury *see* JUDGE.

justice *see* JUDGE.

K

kangaroo *see* ANIMALS.

kettle a clean, shiny kettle is an omen of success, according to gypsy folklore, possibly due to its importance in gypsy culture.

If you are waiting for a kettle that never boils, you may be feeling frustrated that events in life are not happening quickly enough for you.

key this is a powerful dream image and can denote several possibilities:

It can symbolise the solution to a problem, by opening up a BOX, DOOR, or GATE. If the key does not fit this means that you are frustrated at your inability to find the answer.

Keys can also mean that you are keeping emotions or secrets 'locked away'. If you open the door, gate, etc. this means you would like to be more open with your feelings.

A key and LOCK can also have sexual symbolism, i.e. the penis and vagina.

If you give a key to someone else this is a sign of marriage or commitment; if you given a key then the giver trusts you and you should feel confident. However, if you lose a key this means someone will be angry with you.

A bunch of keys can symbolise money, or perhaps a JAILER, depending on the context.

According to the Chinese, the key stands for prudence, and it is a symbol of knowledge in the Bible.

kidnapping if you dream of being kidnapped, it may be that you feel out of control of your life, or swept along by events. If you co-operate with your captors you may want someone to take control of a part of your life.

If you are the kidnapper, this signifies a desire for power.

killing this is a common dream image (*see* section on TYPICAL DREAMS, page 27), and can be very distressing. However, it is unlikely that you wish to kill or be killed. There are several reasons for this dream:

If you kill someone else then they may simply represent a characteristic of yours that you wish to 'kill off', e.g. greed, jealousy. it is worth examining how you feel about this person and what this says about you.

Killing or *murdering* may also symbolise a desire to bring hidden feelings to the surface. These may be sexual feelings, or just strong emotions.

If you dream of being killed you probably feel oppressed and unable to escape a current situation.

king a king in a dream undoubtedly represents an authority figure in your life such as your boss or father. Being summoned to the king means that you desire recognition from this person, although you may fear them too. *See also* QUEEN, THRONE.

kiss if you are kissing a friend, lover or relative, this is a sign of happiness and good relationships.

If you kiss someone goodbye, this denotes a new start in your life (but not necessarily a new relationship).

If you dream of kissing a stranger, this means you may be acting impulsively in some area of life, but things should work out well for you.

If you or your partner is kissing someone else, you may be wishing to end the relationship, or worrying about the possibility of adultery.

Dreaming of 'air' kissing signifies insincerity.

kitchen *see* HOUSE.

kite the symbolism here is obvious: you probably wish for more freedom or to 'go up in the world'. You should be successful, but the string breaking denotes trouble.

kitten *see* ANIMALS.

knave if you dream you are a knave, this foretells of material success. If you see a knave, this is a warning of money troubles.

kneeling if the dreamer is kneeling it may symbolise a feeling of humility or worthlessness. If someone is kneeling for the dreamer, this may suggest the dreamer's power (or desire for power) over the kneeler. *See also* BODY, LYING DOWN.

knees *see* BODY.

knife this is usually a sign of aggression. If you are carrying or brandishing a knife, this means you wish to harm someone (although not always physical harm).

If you threaten to use a knife to hurt someone but cannot carry out your threat, this means you feel useless or inadequate.

Knives also represent the phallus, or the male libido.

If you dream of someone else carrying sharp knives, beware of enemies.

Dreaming of a *knife-grinder* or *knife-sharpener* is an omen of robbery.

See also KILLING, WEAPONS.

knitting this is a symbol of the home and contentedness, but also, according to gypsy folklore, a warning to disregard idle gossip.

knots these may represent problems or questions which you

knots

seek to solve or understand. You may be confused regarding your feelings. If you undo the knot(s) successfully, this means you will find a solution.

Stress could also be symbolised by knots.

According to gypsy folklore, knots symbolise embarrassment and difficulty.

L

labour *see* BABY.

labourer this is a good omen in a dream, symbolising joy and material success, as long as you are careful and do not waste money.

ladder this is a symbol of ambition and advancement.

If you climb the ladder, you are keen to succeed in your career, and you also acknowledge there will be obstacles to overcome.

If you dream of climbing down the ladder you may not achieve the level of success you had hoped for.

Some dream interpreters believe the ladder is a symbol of the male erection.

See also CLIMBING, HILLS.

lake this is normally a calm area of water, so dreaming of a lake means calmness and contentedness.

If the water on the lake is choppy, however, this means trouble ahead. *See also* POND, WATER.

lamb *see* ANIMALS.

lamp *see* LIGHT.

lantern lantern signifies leadership or truth. In the tarot system of symbols, the meaning is wisdom.

If you dream of carrying one to light your way on a dark or

rainy night, then this is a good omen of prosperity.

If the lantern blows out or grows dim, then this means money troubles.

lark *see* BIRDS.

laurel laurel wreaths are still used in real life to hang round the neck of the winner of a race or contest; in a dream they mean a pleasurable victory.

law, lawyer the law or a lawyer is said to be a symbol of a bad business deal which will lose money. Be careful, therefore, of entering into a contract.

See also JUDGE.

leaflet handing out leaflets or 'flyers' denotes a desire to be heard. To read a flyer which has been handed to you means that you will work hard but gain little.

leaves if you dream of fresh green leaves on a tree, then this is a sign that a future business venture will be successful. It also means a change of direction in your life, a new start.

If the leaves are brown and withered, this means money losses or a lack of productivity in business.

If you dream of FRUIT or BLOSSOM with leaves, this is a sign of marriage.

Falling leaves symbolise the past and leaving old ways behind.

See also TREES.

leeches these were said to symbolise illness and medicine in the times when they were a popular remedy for curing disease.

Nowadays they may symbolise something distasteful or frightening.

leopard *see* ANIMALS.

leper if you dream that you have become a leper, this may predict illness, according to gypsy folklore.

You may also feel like an outcast from society due to something you have done, or are believed to have done.

letter Letters are believed to symbolise feelings or the subconscious. If you dream of a letter that you have not opened, this means that you are not acknowledging these feelings. If you open the letter, then you are trying to 'get in touch' with your feelings and listen to your subconscious.

An unopened letter or clean sheet of white writing paper is also said to symbolise sexual immaturity or virginity.

According to gypsy folklore, if you dream of writing or receiving a letter, this is a good omen.

See also PAPER, WRITING.

liar *see* LYING.

library this may mean that you wish to be more educated or learn a new skill. You should be successful in a future venture to further your education.

lifeboat you may feel stranded and in need of rescue from a particular situation.

According to gypsy folklore, you will be successful in a current venture, but success will only be apparent at the last moment.

See also BOAT, LIGHTHOUSE.

light This is generally a good omen, symbolising knowledge and truth. A *lamp* in particular is a sign of truth and goodness in religious art.

If you hold a bright light or lamp in your hands, this denotes a good life, many honours, and success in future ventures. it is especially lucky for lovers or young children to have this dream.

lightning

A dim light or lamp means sickness, and a light that is extinguished or that goes out means danger or death.

If you dream you are on a boat and see a light in the distance, this means you should achieve your desires.

If you dream of an *illumination* of some sort, this is an omen of great happiness.

See also CANDLE, LANTERN.

lightning lightning can symbolise the proverbial light-bulb above the head: a great flash of inspiration, a sort of 'brainstorm'. You may solve a problem which has been puzzling you.

Traditional interpreters say that thunder and lightning foretells of war and trouble.

See also STORM.

lighthouse this is usually a warning symbol: be careful you do not make silly mistakes or rash judgements. Listen to people around you and take their advice.

You may also feel that you are adrift and need assistance.

See also BOAT, LIFEBOAT.

lily *see* FLOWERS.

limping if you dream that you are limping this may mean you have done something shameful, or you have been unlucky recently. You may also feel run-down.

linen clean, fresh linen symbolises good luck and happy news. Dirty linen means you will be disappointed, unhappy, or suffer money troubles.

lion *see* ANIMALS.

lizard *see* ANIMALS.

load if you are carrying a heavy load in your dream, the symbolism is obvious: you are feeling weary, or have taken on a heavy burden in waking life. If, however, you get help with carrying, note who it is that helps you, as they may be a valuable friend. If you manage the load successfully to your destination, you should overcome any difficulties.

loaves *see* BREAD.

lobsters *see* FISH.

lock this signifies a difficulty in achieving a goal, according to gypsy folklore.

A **key** and lock can also symbolise the penis and vagina, and therefore this may be a dream about sexual desire.

locomotive *see* TRAVEL (TRAIN).

locust *see* INSECTS.

logs if you dream about chopping logs, this is said to predict a visit from a stranger.

looking if in your dream you are looking at the action rather than taking part, this means you feel detached from life at present and need to be more proactive. Maybe you feel that someone is shutting you out of their life.

It may also mean that you have great dreams and plans but are probably confused about these at present.

looking glass *see* MIRROR.

loss if you lose something in a dream, you may be feeling a loss in some area of your life. Perhaps you feel that your youth and energy has gone, or maybe a relationship or friendship is waning.

It could also symbolise missed or lost opportunities, such as a job you regret not accepting.

If you dream of losing your wedding ring, you may be

neglecting your partner, or feel that they are not paying you enough attention. If you find the ring again, you wish to do something to improve the marriage and feel that there is hope of doing so.

According to gypsy folklore, if you are a man and you dream of losing your shoes, this means that someone will be angry with you.

lost (direction) if you have lost your way, you are probably feeling confused as to which direction your life should be taking.

You may also be confused about your feelings towards a particular person. Note if anyone else is in the dream and what they are doing. Are they helping you to find your way? Are you relieved to see them?

love it can be confusing to dream of being in love, and difficult to analyse. You could be happily in love and your dream is simply a reflection of real feelings. You may be in love with someone but not admitting it to yourself. Or perhaps you wish for more love in your life and your dream is a wish-fulfilment fantasy, playing a scenario as you would like it to be. You should examine the context of the dream, including the other people in it, whether your love is reciprocated, whether there is jealousy involved, and so on.

Dreaming of your love being rejected is usually not an omen but a reflection of a worry that most people experience.

If in your dream your friends express your love for you, then you will be lucky and successful.

luck if you dream of good luck, you may feel that you have been 'too lucky' recently and should be careful that your luck does not run out.

luggage this may symbolise a weight that you are carrying around with you on your conscience, perhaps due to something that happened in the past.

lute this is a fortunate symbol, predicting prosperity, good friends and happiness.

lying if you dream of telling a lie, this may be due to an actual lie you have told recently, or a dishonest action which makes you feel guilty.

If you are accused of lying in a dream, this means that you may be making money through dishonest means.

According to gypsy folklore, if your job involves lying, then dreaming of lying is a good omen. It is not certain which jobs are included in this category!

lying down this may suggest laziness or denying one's responsibilities. *See also* KNEELING.

lying in bed *see* BED.

lynx *see* ANIMALS.

M

machine a machine represents a driving force or an energy. It can mean a physical force, e.g. the heart, lungs, limbs, or your health in general. It can also mean a mental or emotional energy: your ambitions, desires, feelings or intelligence.

If the machine in your dream is performing well then this should mean that the above energies are healthy, and functioning as they should. If the machine is under-performing or broken, you may need to pay attention to your health or emotional well-being.

maggots *see* INSECTS.

magician according to gypsy folklore, this means you will receive a surprise soon.

It may also mean that you are suspicious of someone's strange behaviour.

magnet this could be a warning dream, telling you to watch out for traps or tricks.

Traditional interpreters believe that dreaming of a magnet means you are attracted to someone and are planning to make them attracted to you too!

magpie *see* BIRDS.

mail *see* LETTER.

malice surprisingly, gypsy folklore says that someone bearing malice or a grudge against you is a good omen, foretelling of promotion and great honour. Modern thinking suggests that you are concerned as to how this person feels about you.

mantle *see* CLOAK.

map if you dream of reading a map this is an obvious sign that you are looking for direction in life.

If you examine the map and it seems clear, this means your direction is well thought out and you may move house or job soon.

If the map is confusing, you are unsure of the direction you wish to take. Note if anyone else is in the dream, helping you or making you more confused!

maple *see* TREES.

mare *see* ANIMALS (HORSE).

marigold *see* FLOWERS.

mariner *see* SAILOR.

market gypsy folklore states that this means you will profit from meetings with strangers. This interpretation is due to the traditional gypsy way of life in which the market held an important place.

marriage this often symbolises the desire to be married yourself, or to have a partner in life, or maybe just curiosity about what marriage would be like for you.

Marriage could also represent two different parts of your personality or soul – maybe contrasting qualities in you such as kindness and assertiveness.

See also BRIDE/BRIDEGROOM, WEDDING.

Mars if you dream of the planet Mars, this symbolises trouble and arguments with someone close to you soon.

marsh if you dream that you are walking in a marsh, this means trouble in the future. They signify difficult times and sadness.

According to gypsy folklore, dreaming of wading through a marsh with no hope of getting out means that no matter how hard you work, life will be difficult.

If you manage to get out easily, there is hope of a more comfortable life.

See also QUICKSAND, SWAMP.

martyr Dreaming of being a martyr could mean that you are letting someone take advantage of you. – Gypsies believe, however, that it means you will receive praise and approval from those around you.

mask a mask represents the face or persona that you present to the world. What lies behind are the feelings or characteristics that you keep hidden. It can also symbolise a 'brave face' that you have to put on, e.g. if you are dealing with a crisis or bereavement, or facing an adversary.

If you are wearing a mask in your dream, this means you feel unable to show certain feelings, or reveal a particular part of your personality. You may also have a deep secret.

If you dream of someone you know wearing a mask, then you feel unable to get to know the real person as they are holding something back.

If you attend a masked ball or gathering, this symbolises a desire for more mystery or adventure in your life. Perhaps you are even looking for a new love.

mastiff *see* ANIMALS.

mat *see* DOORMAT.

mattress this can mean that you are relaxed and contented with your life at present, or that you are taking a laid-back approach to deal with a particular situation.

A mattress can also represent your BED in the sense of standing for what you have made of your life ('you've made your bed...').

See also FURNITURE.

maypole According to gypsy folklore, this symbolises love and your current partner.

The origin of the maypole goes back to pagan times, where it is said to have been used for sex-worship! It may also be a phallic symbol, according to Freudian dream analysis.

meadow if you dream of walking through a lush, green meadow, this foretells of happiness and prosperity.

medal this means you feel that you should have been praised for something you have done recently. It may also mean that you do not deserve this praise, and your conscience is telling you in this reverse way not to be proud of what you have done.

medicine you may be feeling physically run-down and in need of rest and relaxation.

If the medicine tastes bad or is hard to swallow, this foretells of pain or ILLNESS.

See also HOSPITAL, OINTMENT, PILL.

melon *see* FRUIT.

menstruation if you are a woman of menstruating age and you dream of menstruation, you may be worrying about, or hoping for, pregnancy. You may also have experienced health problems relating to menstruation, or the ovaries, womb, etc.

If you are a woman who no longer menstruates and you dream of menstruation, you are probably conscious of ageing and losing fertility.

If you are a man dreaming of menstruation, you may be

conscious of your partner's health, or it could represent a desire to get in touch with your feminine or creative side.

midwife dreaming of a midwife is possibly due to an actual pregnancy and worries about labour.

It is also said to be a symbol of secrets which are about to be revealed.

See also BIRTH, HOSPITAL.

milk if you dream of drinking milk, this can symbolise happiness and comfort. It can also mean a desire to be comforted by your mother or another important female in your life.

Milk can also represent semen in a dream, so signifying sexual desire, especially when dreamt of by a man.

According to gypsy folklore, selling milk in a dream means you will be let down by a lover or someone with whom you have a close relationship.

If you milk a cow this denotes good luck and success.

mill seeing a mill or *miller* foretells of success and happiness.

mirror dreaming of yourself looking in a mirror can mean that in waking life you are vain and overly concerned with your appearance. If your reflection is not pleasing, e.g. you look old or tired, you may be concerned that you need an image change or a rest.

If you are married and look in a mirror, this could signify children, either your own children or a desire to have some. This interpretation stems from the idea of children looking and acting like their parents.

According to legend, dreaming of seeing yourself reflected in water is an omen of death.

miser If you dream that you are a miser, you may be acting selfishly or meanly.

If someone that you know is the miser, you may feel that they are not acting generously, either with money, or time, or some other commodity.

According to gypsy folklore, seeing a miser in your dream is an omen of bad luck where money is concerned.

mistletoe legend says that this is a lucky plant. If you dream of mistletoe it is a sign of happiness and good health.

money like JEWELS, money can represent whatever is important or precious to you. This can include your power or authority, your desirability, your relationships, or your creative ability.

If you dream of losing money, this may mean that you are concerned about weaknesses in any of the above areas, or you are losing control over your life in general.

If you dream of being a generous benefactor, this is likely to mean that you wish to help others less fortunate than you.

monk *see* PRIEST.

monkey *see* ANIMALS.

monster children often dream of monsters. This is because monsters represent something we FEAR and do not understand. For adults this can be anything from an irrational phobia, a deep-seated fear of death, to a fear of rejection by a lover. The monster image should be examined in the context of the rest of the dream to find out the source of your fear.

See also GIANT, OGRE.

moon the moon represents mystery, success, romance, or that which seems difficult or impossible for you to attain. It can also represent health/illness.

If you are a single woman who dreams of the moon, it foretells of marriage. If you are a woman and you are married or in a relationship it predicts the birth of a beautiful baby daughter.

If you are a married man dreaming of the moon, this means you will have a beautiful baby son.

If you are a criminal or you have just done something to be ashamed of, you will be found out and brought to justice.

If you are admired for your beauty in waking life, the moon foretells of further admiration and great honours.

Dreaming of the moon when you are unwell is a warning of death (not necessarily your own).

The moon can have many appearances and they have individual meanings:

bright, clear moon: if you are a woman, this means you will be in good health and find love. If you are a man, this predicts success in money matters.

clear moon becoming hidden (by clouds): this means unhappiness and bad luck in the future.

dull moon: this is said to warn of a dangerous journey, especially if you are travelling by boat. It can also mean that a wife, sister or other female relative will become ill, or even die. You may also suffer from eye trouble or problems connected with the brain.

halo of light around moon: you will be forgiven for something, or saved from a particular situation, by a woman.

hidden moon becoming clear: this is a sign that you will be successful (if female) or happy (if male).

new moon: this is a good omen, meaning success in your career or business.

red moon: this means you will go on a journey soon, perhaps some sort of mission.

two moons: this foretells of success and an increase in authority or power.

waning moon: this is said to mean that an important man you know (or are familiar with) will die.

morning glory this is a symbol of hope, and predicts happiness for you. It represents the resurrection of Christ.

mosquito *see* INSECTS.

moss gypsies believe that this means you will make money and save it.

mother *see* FAMILY.

moth *see* INSECTS.

mountains these may symbolise difficulties that lie ahead, or potential problems. If you scale the mountains successfully you should overcome these problems

See also HILLS, CLIMBING, VIEWING POSITION and section on TYPICAL DREAMS, page 27.

mouse *see* ANIMALS.

mouth *see* BODY.

mud if you dream of mud and you are disgusted by it, this possibly represents similar feelings you have concerning sex. You may also feel guilty about sex or sexual desires.

If you see yourself covered in mud this can symbolise disparaging remarks which will be made about you by your enemies. It can also mean that you are depressed.

If in your dream you sink into mud you probably feel unhappy due to a lack of control over your life. Perhaps someone else is also exerting power over you and you feel helpless.

See also **quicksand.**

mulberry tree *see* TREES.

mule *see* ANIMALS.

murder *see* KILLING.

mushroom if you dream that you are eating mushrooms, this is an omen of illness, death or dangerous times.

music if you dream of being able to play beautiful music, this may be wish-fulfilment. You may wish either that you could simply play music well, or that you could be more creative in some other area, e.g. art, writing.

If you dream of hearing beautiful music being played, this means you will hear happy and unexpected news soon.

Tuneless or harsh music symbolises bad news.

See also **orchestra.**

N

nakedness this may symbolise a desire to shed inhibitions and show people a different side to you, but be careful as you may go to dangerous extremes in waking life.

Your dream may also be saying that you should be more open and honest with your emotions.

Nakedness may of course have a sexual symbolism, or it may be accompanied by fear of everyone seeing your faults clearly, and rejecting you.

Ancient dream interpreters believed that being naked in a dream was a particularly bad omen, foretelling of sickness and failure. The modern interpretation is now preferred.

See section on TYPICAL DREAMS, page 27.

neck *see* BODY.

necklace – this is a good omen, predicting praise, and success in money matters. However, if you break the necklace, this means bad luck will soon follow.

See also **gems, jewels.**

nectar if you dream that you are drinking nectar, this means you will have a happy, long and prosperous life, according to gypsy folklore. The symbolism here is obvious: nectar was said to be the drink of the gods and therefore very fortunate.

need if you dream that you are in need of something, then this can mean the opposite: that you have actually saved sensibly and you are conscious of the fact that you must keep doing so.

Of course, it can also mean that you have forgotten to do something important, like paying a bill, or that you are conscious of having been too extravagant.

needles according to gypsy folklore, this means you will argue with someone soon. See also **pins.**

nest if the nest is full of eggs, or if you dream of a bird making a nest, this is a sign that you desire to settle down and have a family. It is also said to mean prosperity and happiness in love.

If the nest or eggs are broken, or there are dead **birds** in your dream, this means you may be feeling lonely, or as if you have failed in some aspect of life.

See also **eggs**.

net if you dream of being trapped in a net, then you are probably feeling trapped in a particular situation, possibly by an enemy who is trying to hurt you or catch you out in some way.

nettles stinging yourself on nettles symbolises sacrifices you will make either to attain your desires, or to win the love of the person of your dreams.

newspaper You are possibly looking for some good news or a happier life, and if the news in the paper is good, you will be lucky. If the news is bad then the reverse is true.

According to gypsy folklore, if you dream of selling newspapers, this means you will work hard but not reap many rewards.

night if the action in your dream takes place on a dark night, then this may mean you desire more mystery or adventure, or maybe to hide away from the world and be anonymous.

If you are walking on a dark night, this symbolises sadness and loss, possibly grief.

If you dream of night suddenly coming upon you, this may represent an enemy or person who means to harm you, or your fear of the unknown.

See also **evening, time.**

night-dress this is a symbol of a good and respectable career, for a man or a woman. However, if you rip it, you may have just done something in waking life that you regret. See also **clothes.**

nightmare these are basically any frightening or disturbing dream, and can often recur, so that the dreamer can often dread going to sleep. Children are susceptible to nightmares as they often find it hard to articulate their fears, and what they are afraid of appears instead as a frightening image.

The most important part of any nightmare is the f**ear** that you feel. This almost invariably corresponds to a fear of something in waking life, although it is usually exaggerated. Therefore if you can work out what you are afraid of by what appears in your dream, such as a **monster**, and analyse it, the rest of the dream will start to make sense. When you know what you are afraid of it often helps to banish the nightmare once and for all.

nine *see* **numbers.**

nobility – if you dream that you are mixing with nobility, this may mean you are too proud or snobbish, and you may suffer for this.

nose *see* **body.**

nudity *see* **nakedness.**

numbers numbers can often mean particular things to you and you only, so you may have to examine your life and habits to find if any have significance. If you have four children, four will be an important number to you; twenty-nine may be your house number or that of a house you wish to buy, and so on. Certain numbers do have general significance:

zero: this is a symbol for the female.

one: this may symbolise being single, feeling complete, total unity with another person, or simply yourself. It could also stand for the phallus or males in general.

two: this can mean a couple, a pair of things, two opposing arguments, a choice between two courses of action, or a healthy balance.

three: this symbolises the basic family unit: a father and mother (or two guardians) and a child. It can also represent the Holy Trinity.

four: this is a stable number, signifying the four seasons, the four elements, four sides to a square, or the typical nuclear family, for example.

five: this is a significant number in relation to the body: we (usually) have five senses, five fingers on each hand, five toes on each foot, and one head, two legs, two arms, making five.

six: this may represent sex, or balance.

seven: this is a spiritual or religious number – seven deadly sins, seven wonders of the world, for example.

eight: this stands for death and reincarnation or resurrection.

nine: this symbolises a pregnant woman.

ten: this symbolises the male (*one*) and female (*zero*) together.

twelve: this represents the twelve months and therefore any yearly cycle.

twenty-four: this is the symbol of a complete day.

numbness this means that even if you work hard, you may not be encouraged by others, or reap many rewards.

nun *see* **priest.**

nurse a symbol of caring in waking life, a nurse in a dream probably suggests that you feel neglected and in need of comfort and love. There may be a sexual element to this dream.

According to gypsy folklore, dreaming of a nurse means that you may become ill or unhappy soon.

See also **hospital, illness.**

nuts if you dream of eating fresh, tasty nuts, this means you will have a prosperous life full of honours.

If the nuts are out of date or taste bad, you will be let down in life.

Dreaming of finding hidden nuts means that you will find something valuable.

See also **trees.**

nutmeg eating nutmeg is a sign of impending illness. Grated nutmeg, however, symbolises success despite difficulties.

O

ocean in ancient times, the ocean symbolised life. The state of the ocean in your dream determines the interpretation.

If the ocean is calm, this is a sign of good luck.

If the ocean is stormy, this means bad luck.

A smooth ocean with no ripples means you will achieve many things, both in relationships and the rest of your life.

oculist *see* **optician.**

offerings if you dream of making offerings or sacrifices to **God** or gods, this represents a longing to be more spiritual and virtuous.

office dreaming of an office is often a sign that you are worrying about work, or office politics.

It can also be a sign that you need more structure in your life.

If in your dream you are sacked, this is probably irrational worry, but could mean bad luck in other areas of your life.

See also **work.**

ogre this can often represent someone in waking life of whom you are scared, or someone who has authority over you. It could represent a dominant parent or boss, or a father figure.

See also **giant, monster.**

oil if you dream of oil this can mean that you want something in your life to go more smoothly, such as a relationship. You are possibly recognising that you have to be the one to do the ointment

'smoothing'.

ointment this is a prediction of **illness**, according to gypsy folklore. *See also* MEDICINE, PILL.

old age this may mean that you are conscious of growing old yourself.

It can also represent knowledge and wisdom, either your own or that of someone you respect.

old woman this is a good omen. If you dream that you fall in love with, and marry, an old woman, this means that you will be successful, but some people may find fault with you.

olive *see* FRUIT.

olive tree *see* TREES.

one *see* NUMBERS.

onions this symbol has several meanings, good and bad.
On the bad side, if you dream of eating onions you may have money stolen from you, or a project will fail.

Eating onions can also mean that you will get back something that you lost, or that was stolen from you. Another meaning is that of a faithful lover.

opal in the superstitions of waking life, as well as in dreams, this stone can mean bad luck. Things may not be going as well as they seem to be.

optician according to gypsy folklore, this is a sign that you have to put right something that is wrong, or to confess to a wrongdoing or mistake.

oranges *see* FRUIT.

orchard if you dream of an orchard where the **trees** are full of **fruit**, this is a symbol of success and prosperity.

A fountain in an orchard is an even better omen, symbolising good company and happiness.

If the trees are bare, however, bad luck is predicted.

orchestra an orchestra playing beautiful **music** can mean that all parts of your life are working successfully and harmoniously. You are probably feeling confident and happy with yourself too.

orchid *see* FLOWERS.

organ hearing a CHURCH organ playing is a sign of success and happiness.

ornaments these are a sign that you may be a spendthrift and should be more careful with money.

ostrich *see* BIRDS.

otter *see* ANIMALS.

oven this can represent the changes and developments that you or other people in your life are going through.

It can also mean a desire to become pregnant or to return to the safety of the womb.

An oven can represent the warmth of the **home**, too.

overboard if you dream of falling overboard this can symbolise an anxiety concerning a particular problem, which may be getting out of control.

It can also mean you will become ill, or lose money.

See also BOAT.

owl *see* BIRDS.

ox *see* ANIMALS (COW).

oyster *see* FISH.

P

packing dreaming of packing means you may be wishing to escape from something, or gain more freedom and independence. You need a change of some sort, either to your life in general, or to your relationship or career. Or perhaps you have been working too hard and simply need a rest.

If you are packing and cannot decide what to take, or you find that the suitcase will not close, this may mean indecisiveness about making these changes, or insecurity as to what lies ahead.

padlock according to gypsy folklore, this means you wish to find the answer to a question that has been mystifying you. If you cannot open the padlock, you feel unable to find an answer and feel frustrated. If you do open it, this means that you should find your answer soon, but do not be too intrusive into the affairs of others.

painting if you dream of painting a house or other building, this means someone close to you may be unwell. It can also mean that you will be successful in a future business project.

If you are painting a picture, e.g. a scenic landscape, you may be building your hopes up regarding business or money and are expecting too much.

See also PORTRAIT.

palace this is a good omen, meaning that you will be successful in money matters, and admired by others.

palm, palm tree *see* TREES.

panic if you feel panic in a dream, then it will relate to an emotion in waking life, such as anxiety. Like in dreams involving **fear**, you will have to examine the feeling of panic in the context of the whole dream to find out what it is that is bothering you. It could be something less serious than the dream suggests, such as worrying that you will wake up in time for an important appointment; or it could be a deep-seated fear that surfaces every so often.

pansy *see* FLOWERS.

panther *see* ANIMALS.

pantomime this could be a warning dream: that someone around you is not who they appear to be and may be deceiving you.

On the other hand, you may be longing for some innocent fun in your life.

paper if you dream of writing paper which is fresh and blank, this can represent thoughts that you cannot articulate, or emotions you keep hidden. It can also symbolise innocence and sexual immaturity, especially if the paper is white.

If the paper has been written on already, it could be that someone is trying to say something to you in waking life but you are not listening or acknowledging the fact. Note whether you can read the writing, and what it says: this is your subconscious trying to get the message through to you.

If you see paper with print (rather than handwriting) on it, this means good luck, according to gypsy folklore.

Paper which is used for wrapping gifts can represent our outer appearance and the 'face' we put on for others. If the paper is showy, then maybe you or another person is being false or too extravagant. If it is plain and dull, you may be concerned that this is how you come across to others.

See also LETTER, WRITING.

paradise this is a very lucky dream image, and means that you and your loved ones should attain whatever they desire in life.

paralysis if you dream that you are paralysed, this usually means that you feel as though you are not in control of your life, or of others' actions, and are helpless to do anything about it.

Another possibility is that this stems from a physical stimulus: your subconscious is aware that you are lying still and in a dreamlike state, and this is translated into an image of paralysis.

According to gypsy folklore, paralysis is a prediction of actual illness. This could also be due to physical stimulus; your body is feeling tired or lethargic, as it does at the start of an illness, and your subconscious recognises this.

parcel this symbol has a similar meaning to a **letter**: if unopened, it represents feelings that you cannot or will not admit to, or emotions that you have not yet acknowledged. If you open the parcel, note what is inside: if a pleasant surprise awaits you, then perhaps you are ready to explore these feelings and it will be easier than you thought.

parents if you dream about your parents together, this is said to represent yourself, and the male and female characteristics which make up your personality. Note whether one parent is dominant in your dream: this may be the side you are conscious of at present in waking life.

According to traditional dream interpreters, your parents can also appear as your conscience, if you have done something wrong and feel guilty about it. This is especially true if your parents are no longer alive, i.e. they are 'coming back' to remind you of what you may have done. Also, if you are experiencing difficulties at the moment, you may feel as if you need the comfort of your father, mother or someone who protects you.

See also FAMILY.

park dreaming of walking in a park is a good omen, meaning that you will have a happy and healthy life.

It may also symbolise a desire to be among nature and escape the confines of daily life.

parrot *see* BIRDS.

partridge *see* BIRDS.

passing bell if you dream of hearing a passing bell, which used to be rung when a **funeral** passed, this means you or a member of your family will become ill. *See also* BELLS.

past there are two main reasons why you dream about the past. The first is that you wish to return to happier, more carefree days (which is how we often view the past). Perhaps you miss people from your past, or wish to be young again.

The second reason is that you have not resolved problems or difficulties from the past, and still have emotions to deal with from that period.

You should note who else is in your dream, as they will help you to work out whether you are just feeling nostalgic, or whether you actually have issues to deal with.

patches (on clothes) if you dream of sewing patches on to clothes, this is a dream of contrary meaning. it predicts success in money matters, and health for your family. Often dreams of thrift mean the opposite, as they suggest that you are conscious that you must put money away and economise, and therefore you save wisely as a rule.

path if the path in your dream is easy to walk on and free of dangers, this means that you are taking an easy route through life and deliberately avoiding challenges.

If the path is overgrown, dangerous and narrow, this means that you are having problems at the moment, and feel that you are going in a very difficult direction through life. If you get to your destination safely, things should work out well for you.

pawnbroker according to gypsy folklore, this means that you will go through hard times soon and have money troubles.

peaches *see* FRUIT.

peacock *see* BIRDS.

pearl this represents tears. You or someone you know ill be crying soon, especially if a wedding is involved.

pears *see* FRUIT.

peas these are a symbol that things will go well for you in your career or business.

pen, pencil if you dream of picking up a pen or pencil to start **writing**, this can mean that you wish to be more creative. It could also mean that you need to communicate more effectively with other people.

According to gypsy folklore, a pen or pencil in a dream is a bad omen for business people, as gypsies used to believe that too much knowledge was detrimental to business.

There may also be sexual symbolism attached to these images, due to the phallic shape.

See also LETTER, PAPER.

penis *see* BODY.

pepper either you or someone close to you will be brutally honest, even if that honesty is not appreciated.

performing if you dream that you are *acting* or performing, this could mean that you feel you have to put on a front or a different persona to the outside world.

If you dream that you perform badly and the audience does not appreciate you, you are probably feeling undervalued or ignored in waking life. Your confidence is probably low too.

perfume if you are aware of smelling pleasant perfume in your dream, this is a sign that you will receive good news.

If you dream of receiving a beautiful-smelling perfume, you should also hear good news; bad news is predicted if the perfume smells unpleasant.

Dreaming of giving perfume to someone else, or making perfume, means good luck.

pest, pestilence this is a prediction of bad luck, possibly illness, according to gypsy folklore.

pets if you dream of owning a puppy, hamster, or other pet, this means that you feel safe and secure when you are among friends.

Dreaming of seeing or longing for a pet means that you desire to start a family.

See also ANIMALS.

petticoat this is said to predict problems and sadness.

pheasant see BIRDS.

photograph these represent the images that exist in your life.
If the photograph is of yourself, note whether the image is normal and happy, in which case this reflects your self-image, or distorted in any way. A distortion will show how you really feel deep-down about your appearance and general image, or how

others perceive you.

If the photograph shows a happy scene from the **past**, you may be nostalgic for happier times.

piano if you hear tuneful **music** being played on a piano, this means that things are going well for you at present.

If the music is discordant, you feel that things in your life are not fitting together as they should.

See also ORCHESTRA.

picture *see* **painting, photograph, portrait.**

pie often a homely image, the pie is likely to mean that you are feeling happy and comfortable, and money matters are successful too.

pig *see* ANIMALS.

pigeon *see* BIRDS.

pillow dreaming of a pillow could mean that you desire more comfort in life.

It could also be a result of physical stimulus, i.e. you have dropped or moved your pillow out of reach.

According to gypsy folklore, this is a prediction of death. Indeed, early Christians believed that burying pillows with their dead helped them to lift their heads.

See also BED.

pill if you dream of swallowing a pill, you may feel that in waking life you feel obliged to do something, and may not necessarily want to do it. If you feel better in your dream after taking the pill, this show that you are doing the right thing.

As with dreams of **ointment**, it can also mean that you are ill or becoming ill, and your subconscious recognises the physical symptoms before you are aware of them fully.

pilot

See also ILLNESS, MEDICINE.

pilot if you dream that you are a pilot, this could be a sign that you want to take charge of your destiny, and probably travel too.

Folklore states that being a pilot in a dream is a good omen, meaning that you are feeling secure and protected.

pincers these mean that you feel you are being picked on, even bullied, by someone near you.

In waking life pincers represent a religious martyr, according to Christian symbolism.

pine cone this is a good omen, according to gypsy folklore. Pine cones represent life and prosperity, so you should be successful if you dream of them.

pine tree *see* TREES.

pineapples *see* FRUIT.

pins these are symbolic of petty arguments, or of someone refusing to agree with you. In general, if you dream of sharp objects, problems are predicted. *See also* NEEDLES.

pipe according to gypsy folklore, this is a symbol of peace, reflection and contentedness. The symbolism probably derives from the Native American 'pipe of peace' image.

pirate you may feel that something or someone is threatening your world, perhaps even in an illegal situation.

You may also be worried about getting involved in something which is not 'above board'.

If you are a woman in a relationship, the pirate(s) may symbolise your partner trying to control you. If you are a man, it may symbolise travel abroad. If you are a young, single woman, you may marry someone of a different nationality.

See also PLANK.

pistol *see* GUN.

pit a pit symbolises things going badly for you or a tragedy occurring. You may experience bad luck in your job or business, and suffer problems relating to money or relationships.

pitchfork in Christian art, this is a symbol of the devil, and it means suffering and bad luck according to gypsy folklore. The exception to this rule is if a farmer dreams of one, in which case it means success, but only through much hard work.

pitcher this is a bad omen is a dream, and means that a future venture may fail or suffer. If you dream that you drop a pitcher, death and tragedy are predicted.

place where your dream takes place can be important. It generally reflects your state of mind. Thus, if you dream of being in a relaxed, exotic, or luxurious environment, for example, this is probably symbolic of a desire to escape normal life and be somewhere more exciting. It could also mean that you actually feel relaxed and contented and are happy with your life.

If you are in a place where there is much noise and confusion, or you feel uncomfortable, you are probably feeling overwhelmed by life and need to slow down.

planets dreaming of planets is a good omen, and means that you should hear some happy news soon.

plank, walking the you probably feel that you are being pushed into something and you feel uncomfortable about it. You may also feel that a friend or acquaintance has betrayed you. *See also* PIRATE.

plants *see* FLOWERS, TREES.

playground dreaming that you are in a playground usually means that you need to enjoy life more.

ploughing like most agricultural dream images, ploughing is a symbol of good fortune. The fertility of the ground and the seed-sowing can also represent sex. *See also* FARM, FIELD, HARVEST.

plums *see* FRUIT.

pole a pole and anything of similar shape is likely to represent sex and the phallus.

pole star this represents loyal friends and commitment. You are happy in a current relationship. *See also* STARS, PLANETS.

police this can mean that you will succeed and be highly praised, as long as you are an honest person in waking life. If not, the police could represent your conscience.

You may also be worried about safety and need to feel more protected.

pond dreaming of a calm, clear pond with lots of wildlife means that you are feeling happy and comfortable at present.

If the pond is dried up, or muddy and overgrown with weeds, you may feel that you are stagnating in life and need a fresh start.

See also LAKE, WATER.

pool *see* WATER.

popcorn this may symbolise a desire to have more fun and be childlike; it can predict a happy surprise.

poplar *see* TREES.

poppy *see* FLOWERS.

porcupine *see* ANIMALS.

porpoise *see* FISH.

portfolio to dream of carrying artwork, etc. in a portfolio, means that you would like your work and talents to be taken more seriously.

portrait if the portrait is of yourself, note how you look in it, as this may show how you regard yourself and whether you like the way you look. If it is of someone you know, you should ask yourself why they are on your mind.

According to gypsy folklore, anyone in your dream who is painted in a portrait will live a long life. They also believe that if you receive or give away a portrait, this means that you will betray someone (possibly from the symbolism of 'giving away' someone you know).

position (in your dream) *see* VIEWING POSITION.

potatoes if you are planting and/or digging up healthy-looking potatoes, this means that you will be successful, but only if you work hard. However, if the potatoes are small or unhealthy looking you may fail in a future venture.

poultice to dream of applying a poultice to a particular area may mean that it is painful in waking life, and the physical stimulus prompts the dream.

It could also mean that you are keen to rid yourself of a particular problem quickly.

poverty Opinions differ as to what poverty symbolises in a dream. It can be a dream of contrary meaning, according to gypsy folklore, i.e. you are worrying about being poor and therefore are taking good care of your finances – saving and economising. Therefore dreaming of poverty is often a prediction of success in money matters.

If you are in dire straits financially in waking life, however, this can be an anxiety dream which actually reflects a real situation. Your subconscious is trying to tell you to do something about it.

Traditional dream interpreters thought that if the rich or highly educated dreamed of being poor, it was an omen of bad luck.

precipice if you dream that you are standing at the top of a precipice looking down, this means that you are worried that you may fail in a current venture or job. It can also suggest that you are scared of making a big change in your life which may be for the better.

If you dream that you are **falling** down the precipice, this means either that you are scared of losing control, or that you are in the middle of a real disaster or problematic situation. You may also have a fear of heights which influences your life. Real tragedy or death could also be predicted by this image.

If in your dream you are stuck at the bottom of the precipice, it is likely that you feel trapped in life, and frustrated by certain restrictions.

See also ABYSS and the section on TYPICAL DREAMS (HEIGHTS), page 27.

pregnancy the pregnancy 'bump' usually symbolises a pressing problem that you must deal with soon. *See also* BABY.

present a thoughtful present on a birthday, at Christmas or any other celebration, invariably symbolises affection between the giver and receiver. *See also* GIFT.

primrose *see* FLOWERS.

prison If you dream of being in prison, you probably feel that something or someone is holding you back or oppressing you. Perhaps you have made restrictions on yourself.

If you dream of someone you know being in prison, you may

feel guilty about your recent actions towards them.

If you see a prison from the outside, this can be a dream of contrary meaning, i.e. things may be hard but you are full of hope and you know that one day things will improve.

See also CHAINS, CAPTIVITY, ENCLOSURE, JAILER, IMPRISONMENT.

prize you may be praised for something very soon, especially something relating to your career.

The alternative meaning is that you do not receive enough recognition for your achievements.

priest to dream of *being* a priest, *nun*, *monk*, or *hermit* signifies peacefulness, together with passion.

To dream *about* one denotes pride, or bad feeling towards the dreamer. This latter definition originated from gypsies, who were not regarded kindly by the clergy in days of old.

procession dreaming of a procession, as with any **celebration**, is an omen of happiness and good luck, unless something goes wrong during the procession.

prostitute, prostitution if you are a woman dreaming about a prostitute, this may mean that you wish to be more sexually adventurous, perhaps with another partner. It can also mean that you are disgusted by sex, and possibly repressed, especially if you remember a feeling of disgust in your dream.

If you are a man and you dream about a prostitute, you may desire sex without involvement or commitment. It can also mean that you find sex distasteful. Alternatively you may have a secret connected with sex or feel that you cannot express your sexuality freely.

See also SEX.

prunes *see* FRUIT.

public house if you dream of drinking in a pub, this may express a desire to meet and socialise more with your friends, and relax rather than working hard. Gypsy folklore suggests that drinking in a pub predicts illness and money troubles.

If you are very drunk in your dream, you may be worried about losing control over your life.

If in your dream you own a pub, this means that you will either gain or lose a lot of money.

See also ALCOHOL.

puddles If you dream of splashing in puddles, this may signify a desire to be more childlike and shrug off responsibilities.

According to gypsy folklore, dreaming of puddles means that enemies or other unpleasant people will make life difficult for you in the near future.

pumpkin *see* FRUIT.

punishment you may dream of being punished as a result of doing something bad or illegal in waking life. This is your subconscious acting as your conscience. This is especially likely if you were brought up strictly.

On the other hand, you may feel that someone is punishing you too harshly or blaming you for something that you did not do.

puppet the symbolism here is obvious: you feel that someone else is 'pulling the strings' in your life and that you are being controlled. The reverse is true if you are the puppet controller and someone you know is a puppet. You should examine your relationship with this person.

purity if you dream of pure air, water, etc. this means that you are feeling happy and relaxed. The reverse is true if the air or water is dirty or smelly.

If you dream of yourself as a pure, innocent person, you may feel that you are inexperienced in life, or that this is how others see you.

purse the purse represents the female and femininity. It generally represents anxiety too. If you dream of a purse it can mean that you are worried or upset about puberty or menopause approaching, or any other female health issue, such as infertility.

According to gypsy folklore, if you find a purse full of **money**, this is a sign of good luck and happiness. If you lose a purse you may become ill in the near future.

puzzle a puzzle in a dream relates to one in real life; or a complex problem to be solved.

pyramid this is a symbol of riches and great power, doubtlessly due to the fact that Egyptian kings were buried here with their treasures. If you dream of standing on top of a pyramid, you will achieve great things.

Q

quail *see* BIRDS.

quarantine dreaming of being quarantined from others is different from **abandonment**, in that there is a purpose to your being alone, and it may be for your own good or for the good of others. You may need to clear you mind, or remove yourself from someone with whom you may have spent too much time lately.

It could also mean that you have done something wrong, and feel guilty, so wish to 'distance' yourself from the wrongdoing.

See also IMPRISONMENT, PRISON.

quarrel if you are quarrelling with someone in a dream, this can mean that you are angry with this person, or that they are angry with you.

It can also mean that you are going through an inner 'quarrel' or struggle, i.e. that you have some feelings or emotions that trouble you.

The more traditional view is that this is a dream of contrary meaning, and that quarrelling with someone in a dream is actually a sign of desire.

See also FIGHTING.

quarry according to gypsy folklore, if you dream of falling down a quarry this denotes an illness or a run of bad luck.

quay this is a sign that you will be protected by others.

If you dream of leaving a quayside, this means that you are making a change in your life for the better, or seriously considering it. You are possibly contemplating travel as a way of making a change.

If you are saying goodbye to others at the quayside, they represent the way of life that you are leaving behind (although it does not necessarily mean that you do not want to see them again).

queen if you dream of seeing a queen in your dream, this is a sign that you will be happy and fulfilled, and praised at work.

If you dream that the queen visits you, she may represent a boss or parent from whom you desire more attention or recognition.

See also KING, THRONE.

quicksand this can be a warning to look out for hidden traps, and things not really being as they seem. You may also be tempted into something, against your better nature. Note who else is in the dream: are they trying to trap you, or helping you to escape? *See also* MARSH, MUD, SWAMP.

quicksilver the symbolism here is obvious: you are going through rapid changes, or may be feeling restless, according to gypsy folklore.

R

racoon *see* ANIMALS.

race if you dream that you are taking part in a race, note who else is taking part. A race can have several meanings:

It can be that you feel that you have something to prove, to yourself or others.

You may have a rival, whom you are anxious to beat or outwit.

It may also symbolise an ambitious nature and a desire to shine and get ahead– at work, for example.

If you lose the race, it could be that you acknowledge that you will not always be the best, or maybe you have an unjustified fear of failure.

radio a radio symbolises communication, or intuitive feelings, especially where a partner or loved one is concerned. If the radio plays clearly, you probably have no problems communicating. If the broadcast is too quiet, or you do not understand what is being said, you may have problems.

rags according to gypsy folklore, this means the opposite, i.e. that you will be successful and happy. *See also* PATCHES.

raffle you may feel that you are leaving too many things to chance, and feel insecure about doing so.

raft you may experience trouble in the near future, but you should not worry as you will be safe and protected. See also

BOAT, TRAVEL.

railway a railway represents the path you will take through life, and changes you may be going through at present. As in a dream of a path, the state of the railway (overgrown, tidy or uphill) determines how easy or difficult it will be. *See also* TRAVEL.

rain Rain may be annoying to many people, but without it, living things die. It is a sign therefore of fertility and replenishment, and a positive omen that things will get better for you, either in business or relationships.

Rain can also symbolise the washing away of trouble or a difficult past. Maybe you also want to wash away guilt of some sort.

If the rain is torrential, there may be underlying problems, even depression.

See also FLOOD, WATER.

rainbow a rainbow is generally thought to be a good omen, in waking life as well as in dreams. It symbolises changes and the future. A rainbow is a particularly good omen for the poor and the sick. Where and when it appears can be significant:

If the rainbow appears to the right of the sun, this means good luck and positive changes for the future. If it appears to the left, bad luck is predicted, although you should not be troubled with it for long.

If it appears directly overhead, this means money troubles should be over soon.

raking this is a symbol of prosperity through hard work.

ram *see* ANIMALS (SHEEP).

rape if you dream of being raped, this is unlikely to mean that you fear being raped, or that you desire to be dominated sexually. It is more likely to mean that you feel that someone is taking advantage of you in waking life, perhaps using threatening behaviour or a dominant personality. Or perhaps someone is being intrusive and interfering in a bullying or dominant way.

If you dream of being a rapist, this could relate to repressed violent tendencies, which may need to be examined, even by a professional counsellor.

If you witness a rape in your dream, this may mean that you feel powerless to stop another person's behaviour.

raspberries *see* FRUIT.

rat *see* ANIMALS.

raven *see* BIRDS.

reading whatever you read in your dream is significant, e.g. a romance, an adventure, in which case you probably desire more romance or adventure in your life. If someone is trying to get your attention but you are too busy reading, then be aware that you may be shutting out someone in waking life. *See also* BOOK.

red *see* COLOURS.

reeds according to gypsy folklore, reeds are a warning that you must be strong and use good judgement if you wish to be successful. This symbolism came about because reeds symbolise weakness in the Bible.

reflection seeing your own reflection represents the way you see yourself in waking life, i.e. your self-image. *See also* MIRROR.

reindeer *see* ANIMALS (DEER).

relics this means that you must take care of things that are valuable to you, or you may lose them, according to gypsy folklore.

religion This could be a sign that you need to ask for help and religious guidance in some matter, or attend your place of worship more often. However, it is not just religious people who dream of religion, and the images you dream about may not necessarily relate to religion or spirituality. For example, dreaming about being in a holy place of contemplation such as a quiet **church** may mean that you need more peace and time for reflection in your life.

God or a religious leader can also represent a figure of authority to whom you may turn for guidance.

See also ABBEY, PRIEST.

reptiles in general, reptiles in dreams are bad omens, denoting arguments or bad luck. *See also* ANIMALS (CHAMELEON, LIZARD, SALAMANDER, SNAKE).

rescue if you dream of being rescued, you may have to 'rescue yourself', i.e. you are acknowledging through this dream that you have problems, and only you can solve them.

According to gypsy folklore, it can also mean that a promotion is on the cards, or a successful new venture.

revenge this is a warning not to overreact or act harshly. You may also be over-stressed at present, and it could make you ill.

rice rice is a symbol of wisdom and knowledge, so to dream of it means that you will receive useful instruction or education. This symbolism is said to derive from the fact that rice was a staple food of ancient eastern sages.

riches *see* MONEY.

riding this can be a good omen, meaning that you will be successful in business. There is also an erotic symbolism attached to riding fast on a horse. *See also* ANIMALS (HORSE).

ring in most cultures and throughout time, the ring has been the ultimate symbol of love and commitment.

If you are single and you dream of a ring, this could mean that you desire to be married.

If you are married already, then dreaming of a ring means that you are conscious of your marriage. Either you are happily married or something has made you question your commitment.

If you are a married woman and you dream that your wedding ring breaks or becomes distorted, this means that your husband or a member of his family may become ill.

If you dream of losing your wedding ring, then you and/or your partner may be neglecting your relationship. If you find it again, all is not lost.

river the river represents your life and what is happening in it at present.

If the water is calm, clear and free-flowing, then you feel contented with life, and should be successful.

If the river is wide and difficult to cross, muddy, or dangerously fast, this means that you are currently experiencing problems and they may be getting out of hand.

See also STREAM, WATER.

road *see* PATH.

robin *see* BIRDS.

rock a rock can symbolise qualities such as stability, good sense and reliability. Maybe these are qualities for which you are known and admired, in which case the rock represents yourself.

Alternatively, if you dream of rocks getting in your way (when sailing, walking, etc.), they represent obstacles in your life. If you get round them easily in your dream, this is a sign that the obstacles in your life will not be too problematic.

rocket this can symbolise a success or achievement which was glorious but did not last long.

Because of their phallic shape, rockets can also symbolise sexual desire.

rod according to gypsy folklore, a rod is symbolic of sadness.

It can also have symbolise the phallus and therefore can mean sexual desire.

roller-coaster *see* FAIRGROUND.

roof *see* HOUSE.

rook *see* BIRDS.

roots (of vegetables, etc.) if in your dream you see long roots, this means that you feel close ties to your family. If short, it may be that you do not know much about your past, or you do not feel close to family members.

Gypsy folklore states that if you dream of pulling up roots and eating them, this means that you are under a lot of pressure and may do foolish things which are out of character.

See also TREES.

rope It is important to note what the rope is doing in your dream.

Seeing a length of rope can symbolise how attached you are to others, and in particular it may symbolise the umbilical cord, i.e. closeness to your mother.

If you are tied up with rope, this represents restrictions in your life.

If you are being led by a rope, this means that you may become involved with someone or something (e.g. a business proposal) which gets you into trouble.

rose *see* FLOWERS.

rosemary if you dream of simply seeing rosemary, this is a good omen. If you smell it, however, bad luck may befall you, according to gypsy folklore.

rouge this is a warning sign that things are not what they seem, and you may be deceived.

rowing this is generally a good omen in a dream, unless you fall out of the **boat**. *See also* OVERBOARD.

royalty *see* KING, QUEEN.

ruins this means that you will come by money through unexpected means.

running this can be a lucky dream, symbolising health and the life force. Gypsy folklore also suggests that the dreamer will have a fortunate journey, or 'go up in the world'.

Alternatively, if the dreamer is running away, the obvious interpretation is that they are avoiding an issue in their life. Whatever is making them run may appear in the form of a monster, evil person, etc.

rust this is a warning to look after the things that matter to you.

rye dreaming of rye is a good omen, as you will be successful and prove doubters wrong.

S

sabre dreaming of this **weapon** can mean that you will be successful and defeat your enemies.

It is also an erotic symbol, according to Freudians.

sack *see* BAG.

sacrifice *see* OFFERINGS.

safe you may be hiding a guilty secret.

sage dreaming of this herb means that you will be successful and gain promotion.

sailing *see* BOAT, TRAVEL.

sailor dreaming of a sailor may mean that you desire to travel, or it can predict a difficult voyage.

salamander *see* ANIMALS.

salmon *see* FISH.

salt salt can represent several things: your enjoyment of life; your attitudes towards, and interaction with, other people; your feelings and emotions; your daily moods. Note whether there is an abundance of salt in your dream, in which case you probably live life to the full. If you run out of salt, you probably do not enjoy life as you should.

Salt can also represent money, and if there is much salt, then you should not have money troubles.

According to gypsy folklore, salt denotes wisdom, your own or that of someone you admire.

sand walking on sand in your dream can mean that you fear that the good things on your life could easily disappear.

Dreaming of golden sandy beaches could mean that you wish to escape ordinary life and be somewhere more exotic.

If you dream of sand in an egg-timer means that you are conscious of time and are probably feeling pressured.

See also BEACH.

satin this is a symbol of prosperity and riches, according to gypsy folklore.

scaffolding you may feel insecure at work or in a relationship, and feel that you need to work hard to put things right.

scarecrow this is a warning that a friend may not be acting honestly, or with your best intentions in mind.

school school can represent your morals and values, as well as the restrictions you impose on yourself. Therefore, dreaming of school may mean that you are suddenly conscious of your morals – perhaps they are being tested at present. Another interpretation is that you are aware that you do not have enough knowledge about a particular thing: it could be your work, or something you are doing to try to impress others. This is especially true if in your dream you do not understand what is being taught in school.

Note who appears as the teacher in your dream – they could be someone who is making you feel insecure about your knowledge, or perhaps they are trying to help you to do your best.

See also EXAMS.

scissors you may feel under threat from someone, or perhaps as if you have been 'cut loose' from the rest of society.

According to gypsy folklore, dreaming of scissors when you are single means that you will get married, but if you are married already, it means that bad luck will befall you.

scorpion *see* INSECTS.

scratch if you scratch yourself is a dream this may be due to physical stimulus from a real scratch, or pain in that particular area.

It can also be a prediction that you will have an accident.

scroll this is a symbol of secrets to be told. If the scroll is a university degree or other award, you desire recognition at work or your place of education.

scythe this is an omen of someone dying. The symbolism is due to mediaeval belief that it represented death.

sea if the sea you dream of is smooth and calm, this is a sign of happiness and relaxation. If the sea is rough or choppy, you will experience problems in the near future, according to gypsy folklore.

searching dreaming of searching for something can mean that you have lost something in waking life. This could be a partner, a friend, your past, a job, etc. It is a common dream after the death of a loved one.

It can also mean that something that you are striving to attain seems impossible.

If you manage to find what it is you were searching for, then you should be successful in achieving your goals or even renewing your relationship.

If you do not find it, this means that you should put your past behind you and move on, or try to aim for different and more appropriate goals. Perhaps you are nervous about finding what you are searching for too.

seed

See also LOSS.

seed seed can represent fertility and **sex**. It can mean that you are anxious to start a family, perhaps conscious of your age; or that you are anxious not to become pregnant, if female.

Dreaming of a seed, in the same way as dreaming of an **acorn**, can represent potential for growth.

According to gypsy folklore, sowing seed is a good omen and means that you will always have enough money, and always be happy and healthy.

seeing for sighted people, seeing is the most important sense in dreams. What you see does not always make sense immediately, but on examining the symbolism of the images, you can piece together a meaning.

If you dream of having sharp, clear vision, this means that your intellect is sharp. If your vision is blurred, however, this means that you may be working too hard and are not functioning at the height of your intellectual powers.

Seeing yourself in a dream may give you a greater understanding of your inner feelings, or your own self-image. Seeing others may help to analyse your relationship with them, or to work out what their appearance in your dream says about you. *See also* FAMOUS PEOPLE.

See also DEAFNESS, SMELL, TOUCH.

sentry you wish to feel more protected than you do at present.

seraphim *see* ANGEL.

serpent this is said to represent temptation and wickedness, due to the serpent's role in the Garden of Eden. Modern and 19th century interpreters say it is a warning of dangerous enemies, and if you kill the serpent then you should triumph over them.

Freud and other psychoanalysts agreed that the serpent was

a symbol of **sex.**

Much further back in time, dream interpreters such as the Ancient Egyptians said that it symbolised wisdom, the sun and infinite time. If it was seen twisted around a staff, it represented health.

See also ANIMALS (SNAKE).

servant if you dream that you employ a servant, this means that you may be taking advantage of a person's generous nature. On the other hand, it could simply mean that you need to rely on good and loyal friends at present.

If you dream that you are the servant, you could be trying too hard to please others. Note who your employer is in the dream.

According to gypsy folklore, having several servants could mean that you have enemies of who you are unaware. If you hear them talking, this can mean that malicious rumours are being spread about you.

seven *see* NUMBERS.

sex most people dream about sex at one time or another. It is one of life's basic forces, and we need to procreate in order to survive. However, because it is such a basic desire, many people feel that it is not logical or sensible, and therefore 'wrong', to have such 'primitive' feelings. Conditioning and a strict upbringing often mean that sex is viewed as something shameful. You may feel uncomfortable discussing sex, or even thinking about it. Thus, your sexuality, sexual desire, fantasies, etc. are usually hidden and repressed. Dreaming about sex is a way to express these desires. Your imagination can be as free as you like with no need for embarrassment.

If you feel a sense of disgust while dreaming about sex, this may cause you to try to ignore the dream itself. Instead you should look at it as a way of exploring your feelings, and you may learn more about yourself. Dreaming about **insects** and feeling disgusted can also represent your feelings about sex. Again, realising this may help you to understand your inner feelings.

Many objects can represent the phallus, even such things as a **rocket** or a **ladder**. The female sex organs can be represented by a **tunnel,** for example.

Dreaming about sex does not always symbolise sexual desire. If you see yourself being overtly sexual, this may simply be a desire to be more confident and extrovert.

See also HOMOSEXUALITY, PROSTITUTE.

shamrock according to gypsy folklore, this is a symbol of a long life and good health. It is also said to symbolise **travel** by **boat.**

shark *see* FISH.

sheaves this is an omen of good luck, according to gypsy folklore.

sheep *see* ANIMALS.

shellfish *see* FISH.

shelter if you dream that you are looking for shelter, this means that you are having problems and need to take a break and stand back from the situation in order to solve them.

If you are sheltering from the rain, this means you may have a problem of which you are unaware at present. If there is a **storm** and you manage to find shelter from it, this means that you may be very unhappy or angry in the near future, but your troubles should disappear as soon as they arrived.

According to gypsy folklore, if someone refuses to give you shelter, this means that you may be momentarily disappointed or let down, but you will be happy in the end.

shepherd *see* HERDSMAN.

ship a sailing ship is a symbol of hope and good fortune, according to Christian symbolism. If the ship in your dream sails safely in smooth **water**, then your hopes should be fulfilled. If the water is rough, then you may be disappointed.

Dreaming of being in a *shipwreck* means that you may give up hope soon concerning a particular situation, as you have been plagued by bad luck. If you dream of seeing other people shipwrecked, you will be luckier than them in waking life, according to gypsy folklore.

See also BOAT, SAILING, TRAVEL.

shirt if you dream of a clean, new shirt, this means that you will be successful in business.

If the shirt is torn, this means that you will be talked about in waking life. If you are the one who tears it this symbolises the telling of a secret, or embarrassing behaviour.

See also CLOTHES.

shoemaker dreaming of a shoemaker means that your life will be difficult and rewards will be few, according to gypsy folklore.

shoes dreaming of shoes and boots is generally a sign of good luck and happy times ahead. If you see a new pair of shoes you are likely to travel in the near future, and walking without shoes traditionally means you will have a comfortable life.

shooting this can symbolise aggression, and can mean that you are behaving too aggressively, or that you are worried about the behaviour of someone you know. It could also represent a real life attack that you or someone close to you has experienced.

If in your dream you are shooting game and you hit your target, this means that you will be successful in a project in the near future. Hitting a bird of prey means that you will prove your enemies or doubters wrong.

If you dream of hearing the noise of shooting, you may be concerned that others are saying bad things about you.

See also GUN, KILLING, WEAPONS.

shower if you dream of taking a shower, you may wish to wash away guilt over something, or remove someone from your life. For *shower of rain*, *see* RAIN.

shrimp *see* FISH.

shrinking the most obvious symbolism here is that you feel that you are being ignored or treated as if your opinions are foolish. Alternatively, you may wish to 'disappear' from a certain situation, e.g. if you are caught in the middle of an argument.

shrubs according to gypsy folklore, dreaming of shrubs means that you will be happy and find love.

sickness if you dream that you are sick, in the sense of vomiting, this may point to an actual illness of which only your subconscious is aware. On the other hand, it could mean that you wish to get rid of something unpleasant in your life.

If you dream that you are comforting someone while they are sick, this means that happiness will be yours in the near future.

See also ILLNESS.

sieve this means that you are allowing good things to slip through your grasp, and wasting opportunities.

sight *see* SEEING.

silk dreaming that you are draped in silk, or wearing a silk outfit, means that you will achieve something admirable in the near future and be highly praised for it.

If you dream of buying and/or selling silk, you will make money soon.

See also CLOTHES.

silver in waking life this represent information and knowledge; in a dream it means you will discover something surprising, according to gypsy folklore.

singing to dream of yourself singing alone can be a sign of problems; the singing is a cry for help, or your subconscious trying to tell you something. Likewise if you dream of those close to you singing, they may be asking for your help.

If you sing or perform in front of an audience, this can mean that you desire attention and praise for your achievements.

Hearing beautiful singing (e.g. by a choir or professional singer) can mean that you will hear good news soon.

See also APPLAUSE, MUSIC.

sinking *see* DROWNING, OVERBOARD, WATER.

sirens these mythological creatures, who were known for leading sailors to their deaths on dangerous **rocks,** symbolise difficulties in your personal life.

You may also feel that you are being persuaded to do something that makes you feel uncomfortable.

sister *see* FAMILY.

six *see* NUMBERS.

skeleton this symbol appearing in a dream often means that you have just had a shock in waking life, or received bad news, or perhaps you are frightened of something that will not go away until you face it.

Dreaming of a *skull* on its own means that you will be punished for something bad that you have done.

See also FEAR.

skiing You desire more excitement in your life, and are very

skull

keen to travel.

skull *see* SKELETON.

sky according to gypsy folklore, a blue cloudless sky in a dream symbolises good health and happiness. The more **clouds** there are (especially dark, heavy ones), the less happiness is predicted.

slang you are possibly trying to fit in to a particular group by acting like the members of the group.

Slang is also a prediction that you will have a very enjoyable experience soon, but may regret it later.

slave according to gypsy folklore, dreaming of a slave being treated badly means that you will receive unfair treatment in waking life. *See also* SERVANT.

sliding, slipping if in your dream you are sliding by accident, e.g. on a wet floor, you may feel as if events in your life are moving too quickly and that you are losing control.

If you deliberately slide on ice, etc. for fun, this means that you will be successful in a future venture.

If you fall while sliding, an obstacle will appear in your way.

If someone trips you up, beware of a malicious person who may be trying to make a fool of you.

See also FALLING, and the section on TYPICAL DREAMS (FALLING), p.27.

smoke if you see chimney smoke, this is a warning to beware of being too complacent about an achievement: it may have a downside to it.

If you are smoking in your dream, you may be wishing to break from the norm and rebel in some way, especially if you do not smoke in waking life.

smell this can represent intuition. If in your dream you smell a strong smell, this can mean that your subconscious is trying to tell you something important, perhaps about a friend, partner or family member.

See also DEAFNESS, PERFUME, SEEING, TOUCH.

snail *see* INSECTS.

snake *see* ANIMALS.

snow dreaming of snow is an omen of success. According to gypsy folklore, however, if it is snowing during a storm, you will experience hardship in the near future but it will not last long. *See also* RAIN.

soap if you dream of **washing** yourself using soap, this indicates a desire to wash away current problems, or break free from a troublesome relationship. you should feel better about your problems very soon.

soldier If you dream that you are a soldier, you may feel that your life is too ordered or disciplined, especially if you are unhappy in the dream. You probably wish a change of career.

If in your dream you are enjoying being a soldier, it is likely that you need or desire more discipline and feel that your life would be the better for it.

sovereign according to gypsy folklore, to dream of being a ruler means that you may have done something shameful recently. *See also* KING, QUEEN.

spade You will be praised and attain your goals in life eventually, but only after much hard work. *See also* DIGGING.

sparrow *see* BIRDS.

spear the spear is the symbol of Mars, the Roman god of war. Dreaming of one means that your enemies will make life difficult for you, according to gypsy folklore.

Some Freudians believe that it also represents the phallus .
and therefore means sexual desire.

See also WEAPONS.

spectacles you may wish to be seen by others as more
intellectual and thoughtful.

On the other hand, it could be a sign that you are not seeing
or acknowledging that which is right in front of you. You may
also be feeling quite low-spirited.

spice it is possible that you wish to 'spice up' your life and travel
somewhere exotic.

Another meaning is that sadness is predicted, as spice
represents Christ's death.

spider *see* INSECTS.

spinning you have a lot on your mind at present, perhaps
financial worries. This is especially true if you also see many
spools in your dream.

sport if you dream of doing a sport on your own, you are aware
that responsibility for your future lies with you, and you alone.
You may feel lonely and in need of comfort, or perhaps you are
happy being self-sufficient.

If you are playing a team sport, this means that you recognise
the need to communicate with others and seek the help of your
friends and colleagues when necessary. Perhaps you have been
neglecting your friends recently and this is a signal from your
subconscious to appreciate them.

See also GAMES

spring according to gypsy folklore, this is a good omen,
foretelling of happiness and prosperity.

spring flowers *see* FLOWERS.

squirrel *see* ANIMALS.

staff this means that you will travel very soon, possibly with one particular goal in mind.

It may also represent the phallus and therefore sexual desire.

stag *see* ANIMALS (DEER).

stairs if you dream of walking up stairs or *steps*, this means that you are feeling confident and should be successful in whatever you do, including marriage.

stars the saying 'reach for the stars' has relevance here: you are ambitious and want to do well in life. *See also* PLANETS, POLE STAR.

starvation like POVERTY, this can be a dream symbol of contrary meaning; i.e. by recognising the importance of always having enough food, you will be prudent and save money.

However, there is another interpretation: if you are starved in your dream you may be starved of something in waking life, such as love or attention.

See also HUNGER, THIRST.

steps *see* STAIRS.

stiffness dreaming of being stiff and unable to move properly may mean that you are being too rigid in your views, and not considering other people's opinions.

There can also be a physical reason for this: your muscles can go into cramp while you dream. It is not unusual to dream of having 'pins and needles', then waking up to realise that your foot, hand, etc. really has this condition.

sting (by insect) *see* INSECT.

stockings you may be wishing to be more adventurous, if you dream of black stockings.

If the stockings are worn and full of holes, however, you

should watch what you say in the near future and be on your guard against trickery, according to gypsy folklore.

stork *see* BIRDS.

storm you may have major problems soon, but they will not last too long. See also RAIN, WATER.

stranger people who are not identified in dreams very often represent yourself. It is therefore important to note as many details as possible, such as their personality traits, appearance, emotions, etc. This may tell you much about what is happening in your life at present.

straw this is a bad omen, auguring trouble with money and general bad luck.

strawberries *see* FRUIT.

stream If the stream or *brook* you dream of is clear, then this is a sign of success in work or business, especially if it is near your home or workplace.

You may fail in a work–related project if the stream is dirty or dried-up.

See also LAKE, POND, WATER.

struggle a physical struggle in a dream is invariably symbolic of a struggle in waking life.

You may dream of struggling to break free from someone's hold on you, in which case you should note who the 'someone' is: are they holding you back in real life? The person holding you back can often turn out to be yourself, in which case they may appear as a **stranger**, or with your own face.

If you manage to break free from the struggle, you should eventually break free from restrictions.

sugar to dream of seeing or eating sugar can mean that you have fallen on hard times, emotionally or financially, and you are seeking comfort wherever possible.

suicide Dreaming of suicide is not a prediction of your own death or that of someone you know. It may be a sign that your actions in waking life are foolish and will get you into trouble. You should think seriously about making major changes in your life. *See also* DEATH.

suitcase in general, a suitcase means that you may wish to travel and broaden your experiences.

If you dream of travelling with a full suitcase, you will save money wisely.

If the suitcase is empty, you will waste money in the future.

summer, sun summer and the sun mean light and warmth, and they are generally good omens in a dream, symbolising happiness and good luck.

It can also mean that you have feelings of affection towards someone close to you, perhaps feelings that you have not yet acknowledged.

Dreaming of a rising sun is especially lucky, while a setting sun may mean that you are about to enter a difficult period in your life. If in your dream the sun becomes overcast, this means big changes will happen soon.

See also AUTUMN, MOON, SPRING, WINTER.

sundial you may spend too much time dreaming and not enough time being active.

surroundings generally, your surroundings or *environment* in a dream reflect how you feel in waking life.

If your dream takes place in a *warm* environment this is a sign of contentment and security. If it is too *hot*, however, you may be feeling stifled.

swallow

If your surroundings are *cold* or icy, you may be acting coldly towards someone, or vice versa. It can also symbolise a loss of sexual interest.

If all around you is dull and dark, then you are probably feeling as if you are stuck in a rut, even depressed.

Brightness and **light** are symbolic of happy feelings.

See also COLOURS.

swallow *see* BIRDS.

swamp dreaming of being stuck in a swamp means you are very troubled at present; your problems are probably financial. *See also* MARSH, QUICKSAND.

swan *see* BIRDS.

swearing this is a bad omen, meaning that you will make an error of judgement. *See also* BLASPHEMY.

swimming You may be wishing to 'return to the womb', i.e. escape to a safe environment.

If you are swimming strongly and easily in your dream, this means prosperity in the near future. If you get into trouble while swimming, this means extreme money problems. *See also* **drowning, water.**

sword dreaming of carrying or wearing a sword means that you desire power and status, or you have just been promoted and feel proud.

If someone wounds you with a sword, you will be hurt or humiliated soon.

sycamore *see* TREES.

T

table this can mean that you desire a stable home life, or simply to feel more secure than you do at present.

If you dream of a table breaking, you are keen to move house or start a new relationship.

See also FURNITURE.

talking if talking is a key feature of your dream, this represents a need to communicate more effectively with people who are close to you, such as a family member or partner. You may also wish to contact someone with whom you have not spoken for some time.

If in your dream you find that it is hard to get words out, or you are talking nonsense, you are probably feeling isolated from others in your social group, perhaps due to shyness or inability to communicate freely. You probably feel quite misunderstood.

See also QUARREL.

tambourine according to gypsy folklore, this is a symbol of luck and of happy times. This symbolism is due to the fact that the tambourine is a favoured instrument in gypsy culture.

See also MUSIC.

tar dreaming of seeing tar means that you will travel far. Dreaming of tar on your hands, feet, etc. means that you may have problems while travelling.

tassels this is a good omen, meaning prolonged happiness.

tea

tea you may be seeking comfort and rest. Tea may also symbolise money problems.

teapot this means that you will soon make new friends, according to gypsy folklore.

tears *see* CRYING.

teasing if you dream of being teased in a good-humoured way, it usually means that you are popular and confident.

If you feel you are being mocked cruelly in your dream, however, this may mean that you have little confidence, and you believe the things that are being said about you.

If you are teasing someone else, beware of taking others for granted.

teeth *see* BODY and the section on TYPICAL DREAMS, p.27.

telegram you will receive good news and/or visit a foreign country.

telephone the telephone represents the way we communicate with others, effectively or otherwise.

If you are **talking** freely with another person, this means either that you feel confident in your ability to communicate with others, or that you tell other people too much about yourself.

If you have problems talking or hearing, this represents your frustration at your lack of communication skills. It can also mean that you are more interested in the other person's life than they are in yours.

temple *see* CHURCH.

ten *see* NUMBERS.

tent This can mean that you wish to 'get back to nature' or make your life less structured.

According to gypsy folklore, a tent is also a symbol of arguments.

test you undoubtedly feel that you are being tested in real life, i.e. you are being judged by your actions and what you say. You probably feel under pressure, either at work or in a relationship. See also EXAMS and the section on TYPICAL DREAMS, p 27.

thermometer you may feel that a particular situation is 'heating up' and getting difficult to handle.

Alternatively, it can be a sign of actual illness, or perhaps you are feeling too warm in bed.

thighs see BODY.

thimble gypsy folklore says that a thimble means that you may have trouble with employment soon, whether finding it or keeping it.

thirst if you dream that you are thirsty, this probably symbolises a lack of something in waking life, whether emotional warmth from others, or a satisfying job, etc.

If in your dream your thirst is satisfied with clean, fresh water, you should find a solution to your problems soon. If the water is dirty, you are not looking hard enough for a solution, or looking in the wrong place.

See also HUNGER, STARVATION.

thistle see FLOWERS.

thorns these are symbols of problems which will seem to wear you down, but which you will solve after much difficulty. They symbolise Christ's suffering before he died.

thread reels of thread can represent either a secret, or feelings that you do not wish to acknowledge.

If you dream of the thread unwinding, the secret will be told, or you will find the courage to face up to your feelings.

Gold thread means that you will be successful through keeping an important secret.

three *see* NUMBERS.

throat *see* BODY.

throne if you dream of sitting on a throne, you are probably wishing for more power and authority than you presently possess. *See also* KING, QUEEN.

tie seeing a tie or cravat in your dream may symbolise that you wish to be free of a present restriction, especially if you take the tie off.

It may also mean that you have a sore throat, and the physical sensation is turned into an image of a tie.

tiger *see* ANIMALS.

time you may find yourself visiting a different time in your life while dreaming: reliving the recent past, or your childhood, for example. This can indicate either nostalgia for people and places of your past, or unhappiness in the present. Alternatively, you may be wishing to make sense of a past event which still troubles you.

If you dream of moving from one time to another rapidly, and feeling confused, you are probably needing to slow down and take stock of your life.

Certain times of the day can also have individual meaning:

morning: this represents the start of something — a new relationship perhaps, a fresh start in your life, or even your childhood.

afternoon, evening: this is symbolic of something drawing to a close — maybe a relationship or a stressful time in your life. If you feel a sense of calm while dreaming, you are accepting these changes gracefully.

night: this can mean mystery, a desire for anonymity, or feelings of sadness or fear.

    See also CLOCK, EVENING, NIGHT.

tinker according to gypsy folklore, a tinker represents a troublesome person either at work or living near you.

toad *see* ANIMALS.

toadstool this is said to be a prediction of personal growth or promotion, due to the toadstool's ability to grow extremely quickly.

tobacco to dream of loose tobacco foretells of pleasure and fun. *See also* SMOKING.

toiling dreaming of working hard for little reward usually means that you will be rewarded for honest hard work. The only exception is if you are very wealthy already, in which case you may have to work much harder, for less reward, according to gypsy folklore.

tomato this means happiness and fun in the near future; however, it may not last long.

tomb dreaming of a very grand tomb can mean a desire for improved status, or more recognition from friends and family. *See also* CEMETERY, GRAVE.

tools these may represent your desire to be more practical, or to be of more help to someone.

    Tools can also represent the phallus, so it may be a sexual dream.

    If the tool is being brandished as a **weapon**, this is likely to symbolise aggression.

torch

See also HAMMER.

torch if you dream of holding an electric torch to find your way, this symbolises feelings of confusion in waking life, and not knowing where to turn for the answer.

If you dream of a burning torch, this may symbolise passion, anger or pain, or perhaps a deep-seated fear.

See also FIRE.

torpedo you should expect a surprise, even a shock, in the near future.

A torpedo is also an obviously phallic symbol and may represent sexual desire.

torrent *see* FLOOD, RAIN, WATER.

tortoise *see* ANIMALS.

touch dreaming of being touched can mean that you have good communication with others, and are happy in your relationships. This is true if you are happy and comfortable to be touched in your dream.

If you are uncomfortable being touched, you may be feeling oppressed and trapped in a certain situation. You could also wish to distance yourself from someone in your life.

See also DEAFNESS, SMELL, SEEING.

tower you may be feeling isolated and remote from others; whether this is of your own doing or not may be revealed in your dream. Note whether you stay in the tower for the duration of the dream, or make an attempt to come down. This symbolises your desire or otherwise to become closer to others.

If you dream of someone you know in a tower, you may never get close to this person. If you climb the tower to be with them, beware of initial rejection.

A tower may have phallic symbolism too.

toys dreaming of playing with toys signifies a desire to be less responsible and grown-up.

train *see* TRAVEL and section on SEXUAL DREAMS, p.26.

trap you may feel as if someone has trapped you in waking life, perhaps with emotional blackmail..

According to gypsy folklore, you will suffer financial losses.

A *trapdoor* means secrets and mystery. If you are trying to open a trapdoor in your dream, you are desperate to find out someone else's secret, even if it does not concern you.

travel Travel is a very common feature of dreams and often signifies our journey through life. If you travel alone, that may be how you picture your own growth and progress. If you travel with a known companion, that person's impact on your journey will be similar to their impact on your life. If the journey changes from one on difficult ground to easier terrain, then you are probably entering a smoother period of your life, and vice versa.

Dreaming of methods of transport can denote various meanings:

aeroplane: a quick transition between one stage of life and the next

boat: the difficulties (or otherwise) of travel over water can reflect difficulties in the dreamer's life. Smooth water indicates prosperity and rough water indicates bad luck. See also BOAT.

bus: an often uncomfortable and time-consuming journey may reflect your own life, but there may also be fellow passengers with which to share experiences.

car: may be just the most familiar mode of transport and therefore not significant. However, it can be important to note who is driving and how in control the dreamer feels, as this relates to the dreamer's independence. The size and status of the car can also denote desire or sexual power.

cycle: can refer to a difficult phase of life which must be overcome

train: a man's dream of a train is generally connected with sex (re: the Freudian cliché of a train entering a tunnel); when a woman dreams of a train it may be that she wishes to be more powerful. You may also be wishing to meet with someone who lives far away from you.

To travel *abroad* to *foreign countries* often means a desire to be free of restrictions in your present environment. This may involve meeting new people or moving to a different area.

To travel *uphill* usually means a situation will improve, but not without difficulty.

Travelling through a *wood* in your dream denotes obstacles and trouble ahead.

See also ACCIDENT.

treasure *see* EMERALD, GEMS, JEWELLERY.

trees the tree as a dream symbol can represent your whole life.

The *roots* of the tree can represent your childhood, your parents or your ancestors – in other words, your own roots as a person. If the roots in your dream are firm and strong, you probably have a strong sense of your family's past.

Branches represent the directions you have taken, or will take in the future, and decisions you have made. Branches which are strong and far-reaching mean that you are decisive and ambitious.

New *leaves* and *shoots* symbolise new life: either a birth, or a complete change of direction for you. If you dream of leaves falling you are leaving something behind to make a fresh start.

Flowers or *blossom* on the tree can symbolise fertility and the desire for a family, and/or happiness and prosperity.

If you dream of *fruit* on a tree it can represent offspring, or the 'fruits of your labour' i.e. your achievements to date.

Tree *bark* symbolises your own protective outer layer, i.e. only that part of your personality that you show to others, your public façade.

If you dream of a tree actually growing in your dream, this represents your own physical, spiritual or emotional growth.

A dead tree in a dream can mean that someone you know has died, or that a particular relationship has no life in it any more. Certain trees have individual meaning:

apple tree: if you dream of a healthy apple tree, you will hear something pleasing in the near future. If the apple tree is dying, the news will be unpleasant.

cypress: this tree represents sadness, even death, according to traditional interpretation.

maple: this tree is a symbol of virtue and loyalty. According to gypsy folklore, dreaming of the maple means a contented and comfortable life.

mulberry tree: this is a good omen, foretelling of success and increased money or status. In Iran and Italy this tree symbolises riches and good fortune.

nut trees: if you pick nuts from trees and eat the nuts, this means you should be successful where money is concerned, but only after difficulties.

olive tree: this is a fortunate symbol as it means that you will be happy and at peace, and what you desire shall be yours.

palm tree: this is a good omen in a dream, if you are a woman who wishes for a family. If you are married or in a relationship, the palm signifies having children, and if you are single it means you will get married. In Christian symbolism the palm stands for victory, and the palm tree for godliness and virtue. It is known as the Tree of Life in Egyptian culture. According to gypsy folklore, anyone who dreams of a palm tree is lucky as it predicts happiness.

poplar: this is a good omen and means that your desires will be met, as long as the poplar is green and healthy looking. If not, you may be disappointed or let down, according to gypsy folklore.

sycamore: if you are single and you dream of this tree, it is a prediction of marriage. if you are already married, however, there may be rows and jealousy soon.

willow: in dreams as well as waking life, this tree symbolises sadness.

yew tree: this is a good omen, meaning that you will be successful and highly praised.

See *also* BLOSSOM, BRANCHES, FLOWERS, FRUIT, LEAVES, ORCHARD, ROOTS.

trench you may feel as if you are under attack from those around you at present. The trench in your dream means that you are trying to be resourceful and think of ways to solve your problems.

triangle this can represent three people, or the Holy Trinity. *See also* NUMBERS (THREE).

tripod you may be seeking more stability in your life. *See also* CAMERA.

trout *see* FISH.

trumpet this symbolises success, and victory of good over evil. *See also* MUSIC.

trunk *see* SUITCASE.

tumble *see* FALLING.

tunnel a tunnel can symbolise a transition from one part of your life to the next. Note whether the tunnel is brightly lit and signposted, or dimly-lit and difficult to get through. This should tell you whether the transition is going to be easy or not.

A tunnel is also said to represent the female sex organs or the birth process. You may wish to re-invent your image or make a completely fresh start (i.e. rebirth) in life.

turkey *see* BIRDS.

turning if you dream of turning round and round, this means that you are unable to make decisions at this present moment.

turnip this is a good omen, meaning that you will have a faithful partner or be successful with money.

turtle *see* ANIMALS (TORTOISE).

turtle dove *see* BIRDS (DOVE).

twelve, twenty four, two *see* NUMBERS.

U

ugliness it is unlikely that you feel ugly in waking life, but you are probably concerned as to what others think of you.

ulcer you may have a recurring problem which keeps nagging at your mind, and are likely to be feeling stressed.

According to gypsy folklore, an ulcer can mean that problems and ill health are about to be cleared away, as ulcers tend to cleanse the system.

See also ABSCESS.

umbrella you are needing to take extra care of yourself, and protect yourself from enemies. You long for more peaceful times.

uncle *see* AUNT.

underground if you dream of something being underground, this can represent a secret – either your own, or that of someone close to you – or an aspect of your personality that you normally keep hidden.

Dreaming of being buried, alive or dead, is common, and can mean that you feel that everything is getting on top of you.

See also DIGGING, GRAVE.

undertaker this can mean that you are suddenly conscious of death.

Alternatively, you may be doing a job or task that you do not enjoy, one that has perhaps been forced upon you.

underwear

In gypsy folklore this is a dream of contrary meaning, i.e. an undertaker is a prediction of a wedding.

underwear *see* CLOTHES.

undressing dreaming of undressing can symbolise the need to tell a secret or get something off your mind.

It can also mean that you wish you were less inhibited, and more open with your emotions.

You may dream of undressing in a sexual context, in which case you should acknowledge feelings of desire which were previously hidden.

See also NAKEDNESS and TYPICAL DREAMS, p.27.

unicorn this has long been a mythical, fairy-tale symbol in waking life as well as in dreams. If you dream of one it means happiness and enlightenment.

uniform if you dream of yourself and others around you wearing uniform, you may simply be recalling past times within a disciplined environment, such as school, or the army. Note whether you seem happy or sad to be there.

If you are in uniform and others are not, you may need to relax and take yourself less seriously.

If others are wearing correct uniform and you are not, this is a common dream of being the 'odd one out' and stems from basic insecurity over fitting in with other people.

uphill *see* TRAVEL.

urination if you dream of urinating, you may be wishing to rid yourself of an unpleasant problem.

If you are caught urinating in public, you may be worrying that in waking life you are not good enough for a particular task, and will be found out.

If someone else urinates on you or your property, it is likely that they have offended you or acted aggressively towards you in waking life.

urn according to gypsy folklore, this is a sign of death.

V

vagabond this is a sign that you will travel far in the near future, or experience changes at work. *See also* GYPSY, TINKER.

vagina *see* BODY.

valet *see* SERVANT.

valise *see* SUITCASE.

valley walking in a pleasant green valley strongly suggests a need to get away from problems, especially if you live in an urban area in waking life.

The curves of the valleys may also represent the human body, so you may be particularly aware of your own body and its shape at present.

See also HILLS, MOUNTAINS.

vampire you may dream of a vampire as a result of watching a horror film recently, but it does not always represent **fear**. It may mean that someone you know is draining your energy, time or money, or bullying you into doing something against your will.

According to gypsy folklore, you should watch out for dishonest people.

vanishing if something vanishes in your dream, you may recently have lost something in waking life, or missed an opportunity, and cannot explain why.

You may also feel low in self-confidence, i.e. that you could

vase

vanish, and no-one would notice.

This may also be your subconscious trying to deal with someone else 'vanishing', i.e. a bereavement or lost relationship. See also **loss.**

vase you may be placing too much importance on material goods.

vegetables if you dream of eating a plateful of vegetables, you may feel that there is something missing from your life. On the other hand, you may be contemplating giving up meat.

veil you may be acting too submissively, and letting others control your life. The veil can also symbolise secrets and mystery.

veins you are probably conscious of your health at present, and may actually be ill. You may also be nervous about a minor operation or an injection.

velvet you are longing for more luxury and pampering. If you are wearing heavy velvet garments and feeling stifled, you may be taking on too much in waking life. *See also* CLOTHES.

vermin to dream of any kind of vermin means that you are worried about poor health and possibly a lack of hygiene. *See also* ANIMALS (RATS).

victory winning a victory in a dream means success and renewed confidence in waking life, especially if others have been doubting you.

viewing position the position from which you view the action in a dream, and how far away you are, can be significant. This represents the place you hold in others' lives and how you view your own life:

closeness: if you are close to someone in your dream, this represents intimacy or closeness to them in real life; either actual, or desired. If you see things close-up in your dream, this means that you are passionate about your beliefs or principles.

distance: if far away from others, you are either concerned about the distance between you and them, or you wish to be less close – only you can say which one is true. If distant from the action or things in your dream, then you may feel that you are not sticking to your beliefs, or you are losing faith in what you hold to be true.

height: if you are high up and looking down on people or things, then you probably now feel safe from something which once worried or threatened you. It may also be that you feel morally or intellectually superior to whomever you are looking down on. You probably feel successful at present in waking life. Alternatively you may feel that your position of height has isolated you from others. If, on the other hand, you are low down and looking up, this may symbolise a task or project which seems difficult, but which you should carry out successfully. It could also represent people in authority, or those people who you feel look down on you in life, or even God. *See also* CLIMBING, HILLS, MOUNTAINS.

in front or *behind*: Things or people you see in front of you represent the future and things you aspire to. If you look behind you in your dream, whatever you see is probably something you wish to leave in the past, or have done so already. There could also be something you are failing to face up to, especially if a CHASE is involved.

village you are wishing for a quieter life, but less anonymity.

Dreaming of a group of friendly *villagers* means that you will feel happy and carefree soon.

vinegar

See also CITY.

vinegar you may have had a sharp shock recently.

On the other hand, you may be feeling unwell, especially in the stomach area.

vines *see* FRUIT (GRAPES).

violence Violence in dreams, like many emotions, is highly exaggerated and dramatised, in order that the feelings are fully released. You should not worry too much about these seemingly disturbing images. Note how the violence is handled: does someone try to stop it? Do you or someone else try to find a peaceful solution? If so, this means that you are trying to find a mature answer to problems.

If you are violent towards someone in your dream, this rarely means that you wish them physical harm. It usually does mean, however, that you have been angry with them recently.

If you dream that someone else is violent towards you, then they may have been acting coldly or aggressively in waking life, and you are concerned that this behaviour may become worse unless you confront it.

See also AGGRESSION, WEAPONS.

violet *see* FLOWERS.

violin according to gypsy folklore, you will meet like-minded people soon and have fun.

viper *see* ANIMALS (SNAKE).

voices these can represent your conscience, especially if they are telling you what to do. Note whether or not the words are those of someone you know, in which case your subconscious may be trying to tell you to listen to this person. On the other hand, perhaps you have heard enough from a particular person and wish to shut their voice out. How you act in the dream on hearing the voice is important.

Hearing happy voices is likely to mean that you have a contented life at present.

volcano unsurprisingly, a volcano symbolises arguments and trouble.

vomiting *see* SICKNESS.

voyage *see* TRAVEL.

vulture *see* BIRDS.

W

wading if you dream of wading through **water**, things in your life may be moving more slowly than you would like, and you are frustrated by a lack of progress.

If you are wading through **mud**, you may be feeling guilty about something.

walking if you dream of walking with purpose, you have definite plans in mind and will carry them out without help from others.

Walking on a dark **night** means that you are feeling unhappy, even grief-stricken. You may also desire more mystery in your life.

If you dream of walking in dirt or **mud**, you may be experiencing guilt feelings, or an illness.

Walking aimlessly suggests that you do not know how best to achieve your goals.

wall walls represent your own barriers, defences, or self-protection. They stand for all that you do to keep innermost feelings hidden, and to present the face you want the world to see.

If the wall is particularly high, you may be acting too defensively. If too low, you could be telling too many personal secrets.

Dreaming of being surrounded on all sides by walls means that you are either feeling very secure or a little hemmed-in.

If you scale a wall safely and successfully, this is a good sign that you should overcome present problems. If you do not get over it, or see no means to do so, this means either that you have an obstacle in your life which you may feel is defeating you, or you are experiencing problems with close relatives.

Narrow walls mean that you have not made sufficient provision for hard times, and may have squandered money.

See also HOUSE.

walnuts these are a sign that you will experience difficult times soon.

walrus *see* ANIMALS.

waltz you may feel as if you are 'out of step' from those around you.

war this is usually a sign of impending confrontation with those who are close to you, especially family members.

warbling dreaming of BIRDS warbling means that you will be happy, according to gypsy folklore.

wardrobe this can represent either the womb or your sexuality. If you discover something in the wardrobe, you may be finding out more about this aspect of yourself. If it is locked, you may not be ready or willing to explore this. See also FURNITURE.

warehouse according to gypsy folklore, you will save money wisely and therefore avoid money troubles.

warts you may be seeing problems where there are none.

washing *see* WATER.

wasp *see* INSECTS.

watch you may be conscious of time slipping away.

This is also a prediction of a successful venture.

See also CLOCK.

water water is a very common dream symbol, as it is such an important feature in our lives.

If you dream of **swimming** in deep water, this could mean a desire to regress to a womb-like environment, i.e. to feel protected and safe. If you get into trouble while swimming, you may face dangerous problems concerning money or business, in waking life.

Washing usually means that you need to cleanse yourself of problems or troublesome emotions, or to feel more spiritual. It can also symbolise your recovery after an illness.

Walking or *wading* through water means that you are frustrated by a lack of progress.

Drowning or *sinking* in a dream means financial or business problems; or it could be that you suffer from breathing problems in waking life.

If the action in your dream takes place underwater (and everyone can breathe normally), this can mean that you wish for your life to slow down a little, or to get in touch with your spiritual side.

Tidal movements and *waves* symbolise events beyond your control, such as emotional mood swings, or even menstruation.

The *sea* represents happiness and serenity if calm, or major problems if rough.

Dreaming of an *ocean* means you are looking at your life objectively; the ocean represent life in general. A calm ocean means good luck, and a stormy ocean, bad luck. An ocean like a millpond means success.

Carrying water means success and happiness.
See also BOAT, LAKE, POND, STREAM.

water mill this means good luck, according to gypsy folklore.

watermelon *see* FRUIT.

waves *see* WATER.

wax this represents a changeable and even fickle person; someone you have reason to distrust. See also CANDLE.

wealth *see* JEWELLERY, MONEY.

weapons These are invariably a symbol of aggression and hostility, of a physical or sexual nature. Firing weapons may represent the sexual act, while the weapons themselves (**e.g. cannon, gun**) could represent the phallus.

You may, however, be fighting with weapons and winning a battle, which may mean that you have recently overcome an obstacle or problem using bravery and strength.

See also AXE, KILLING, KNIFE, SPEAR.

weather pleasant weather generally suggests happiness and contentment, but do not be too complacent.

Bad weather usually means problems, worries, or even depression.

See also **rain, snow, storm, sun, wind.**

A *weathercock* or *weathervane* represents changeable moods, in yourself or others.

weaving this means that you should be successful in a current project or venture at work.

wedding seeing a wedding as a celebration is a sign of a family get-together or party.

If you dream of the actual service, this may be simply wish-fulfilment. It could also be a symbol of partnership in general, e.g. in business, or a stronger commitment to someone close to you. If a man dreams of the wedding service, he may be anxious either about a wedding in the future or some other partnership.

See also BRIDE/BRIDEGROOM, CELEBRATION, MARRIAGE.

weeding, weeds you will work hard but be rewarded for it.

weeping *see* CRYING.

whale according to gypsy folklore, this is a sign of imminent danger.

wharf *see* DOCK.

wheat this is said to mean money and happiness. *See also* BARLEY FIELD, FARM, FIELD, HARVEST.

wheel this represents anything with no beginning or end, i.e. life, birth, death, rebirth, etc. it is generally a good omen as it means constancy.

Dreaming of a *roulette wheel* may mean that you are taking too many chances in life.

whip if you dream of being whipped, you may feel guilty about something and your conscience is trying to 'punish' you.

If you whip someone else in your dream, it is unlikely that you wish to hurt them physically, but probably feel anger towards them.

Whipping an animal symbolises feelings of failure and sadness.

whirlpool dreaming of a whirlpool can mean that you are getting involved in something dangerous or unpleasant, against your better judgement.

The feelings of being whirled around can also be due to physical stimuli such as a headache or nausea during sleep.

whirlwind you may feel as if you are losing control of your life.

Like a **whirlpool**, a whirlwind in a dream may appear as a result of physical ailments.

See also WIND.

whispering if you dream that you are whispering, this can mean that you are being ignored or undervalued.

If someone is whispering to you, you may have trouble understanding them or accepting their point of view in waking life. Perhaps you do not want to listen to them.

Dreaming of more than one person whispering means that you are afraid that others are talking about you.

white *see* COLOURS.

widow, widower you may worry about losing your partner, or being abandoned by those you love.

wife dreaming of your wife or *husband* is either a symbol of love, or a sign that you are concerned about their health or behaviour. *See also* MARRIAGE, WEDDING

wig you may be concerned about your appearance, or you are trying to hide something.

It can also be a sign that there is more to a particular person or situation than meets the eye, and you should be wary of trusting too soon.

wilderness you are probably feeling isolated and ignored; this could be a warning to be more self-reliant and you will be respected for it.

will you are conscious of your own mortality and feel concern for family who would be left behind. You may also be feeling quite low.

If you dream of the will of someone you know who is still living, this probably means that you do not appreciate them enough in waking life.

willow *see* TREES.

wind this symbolises forces beyond your control, or people who are seen as 'free spirits'. If in a dream you are being blown along by the wind, perhaps it is time to take more responsibility in your life.

Dreaming of looking at a strong wind can symbolise stress and disagreement. A pleasant breeze means calmness.

A *windmill* symbolises good luck.

window dreaming of looking out through an open window means a desire for a change of direction, a fresh start.

If it is impossible to open the window, you probably feel stifled and frustrated in waking life.

Seeing a face outside the window can mean guilt associated with that person.

Dreaming of looking at a brightly-lit window from outside means that you yearn for home comforts.

wine drinking a moderate amount of wine in a dream usually means that you are happy and relaxed in waking life. There may also be a celebration in the near future.

Over indulging could point to a lack of control in your life.

See also ALCOHOL.

wings dreaming of growing wings and **flying** may mean that you wish to escape your present environment, or make more decisions for yourself.

winter it is likely that you feel quite sad or bored at present. *See also* AUTUMN, SPRING, SUMMER.

wire this represents restrictions and being held back from what you wish to do.

witch, witchcraft, wizard dreaming of a witch or wizard means that you are worried about someone else abusing their power.
If you are the witch/wizard, you probably wish that you had more control over a certain person or situation.

wolf *see* ANIMALS.

womb dreaming of returning to the womb undoubtedly means that you crave security and peace. you probably wish to be free of responsibility too.

wood (in the sense of a wooded area) *see* TRAVEL.

wool this is generally a good symbol, meaning that you will be successful and happy at work, according to gypsy folklore.

work dreaming of your workplace probably means that you have problems there, or are stressed from too much work.
If you dream of others working, you should be successful in business ventures.
See also OFFICE.

workhouse if you dream of being in a workhouse, you probably feel that others are taking advantage of you.
Gypsy folklore says that it means you will come into money in a lucky way.

workshop you are willing to work hard to achieve your goals, and are probably more entrepreneurial than most.

worms *see* INSECTS.

wound(s) dreaming of wounds can mean that you have problems from your past which still trouble you.
Wounds can also represent loss of virginity, especially if the experience is not a pleasant one, or menstruation, if dreamt of by a female.
You may also simply be frightened of blood and wounds in

waking life.

wrapping paper *see* PAPER.

wreath a **funeral** wreath can mean that you have recently suffered a loss, or that you are conscious of your own mortality.

A Christmas wreath is probably a sign that you want to spend more time with family and friends.

wreck this symbolises either a recent accident, or a future problem.

wrinkles you may be concerned about ageing and how you look.

You may also be feeling that you have not done all the things you wanted to by this stage in your life.

wrist *see* BODY.

writing this usually means that you desire better communication, or you wish to get in touch with someone whom you have not seen in a while.

According to gypsy folklore, you should receive a letter soon. *See also* PAPER, LETTER.

X

x-ray you feel as though you are giving too much of yourself away. You may also be worried about an impending HOSPITAL visit.

Y

yacht a yacht on a calm **sea** means good luck and prosperity; a stormy sea means problems. *See also* BOAT.

yawning according to gypsy folklore, to dream of yourself yawning means that you may be caught unawares in the near future.

yellow *see* COLOURS.

yew tree *see* TREES.

yoke you feel as if people are taking advantage of your generous (and perhaps submissive) behaviour.

youth to dream that you are younger than you are means that you feel worried or sad about ageing, or feel that you were happier then.

Z

zebra *see* ANIMALS.

zero *see* NUMBERS.

zodiac dreaming of any of the signs of the zodiac can mean that you are interested in broadening your horizons through travel. It could also be that you need inspiration to guide you through life.

zoo a zoo can represent your family environment or your peer group. If you dream of being contented while in the zoo, you are probably happy with things the way they are. If the inhabitants seem restless or unhappy, this may be the way you feel; perhaps you need time away to be on your own. *See also* ANIMALS

GLOSSARY

brain waves these control the way your brain works in its different states of activity. There are four types:

beta: these control the brain in an alert state of wakefulness.

alpha: these are present while you are still awake, but feeling more relaxed.

theta: these control the brain when you are deeply relaxed, e.g. the first stages of sleep.

delta: these occur in the deepest stages of sleep.

conscious the part of your mind that is aware of your self, your environment, etc. It will determine most of your actions while awake. Compare subconscious, unconscious.

déjà vu a feeling that you have 'been here before' and that the events you see in waking life have already taken place in your dreams. See the entry for DÉJÀ VU in the list of symbols.

free association a method of psychoanalysis developed by Sigmund Freud. The idea behind it is to associate words, suggested by the psychoanalyst, with other words or images in your mind, in a free-thinking, spontaneous way. This can be used in a variety of therapies but also helps to analyse dreams and their meanings.

Freud, Sigmund (1856 – 1936) a highly influential Austrian neurologist. He was credited with the invention of psychoanalysis, the treatment of mental disorders by **analysing**

the unconscious mind. Other areas of development included free association, psychosexual behaviour and the power of the subconscious.

insomnia the inability to sleep for a long enough period, or to get to sleep at all. It can be caused by stress and worry, or illness. See also WHAT HAPPENS IF I CAN'T SLEEP? on page 19.

latent content this is the hidden or implied meaning, the symbolism, behind the manifest content in your dreams.

manifest content the actual obvious content of the dream, i.e. what happens in it. What is represented, or symbolised by this is the latent content.

oneiromancy the traditional name for the study and analysis of dreams.

REM sleep this stage is entered after sleeping for about 90 minutes, and is where you do most of your dreaming. Your muscles will probably be in a sort of paralysis, to avoid them moving about while you are dreaming.

subconscious the part of your mind deeper than the conscious. You are not normally aware of subconscious thoughts but they can be accessed easily if necessary.

symbolism the expression of messages, , thoughts or emotions without spoken or written language. Symbolism is all around in waking life (think of traffic lights or semaphore, for example) and also in dreams. It is what dream analysts have examined for many centuries in order to analyse the meanings of dreams and predict the future.